"When as a novice I first began not many years ago to sketch and paint, I discovered not only an avocation—but a calling to see in a whole new way. That is what Juliet Benner's beautiful book does—helps us to see God's story with freshly cleansed eyes. *Contemplative Vision* is a guide that deeply engages the mind and heart and imagination. It takes us into the transforming presence of the God who unveils himself in Scripture as seen through the eyes and hands of gifted artists. Do read—and gaze—and see for yourself!"

Leighton Ford, president, Leighton Ford Ministries,
and author of *The Attentive Life*

"In this creative guide to prayer and meditation, Juliet Benner draws from the deep wells of Scripture and art appreciation, guiding us toward spiritual transformation. Benner has shaped an important resource for Christians, especially those interested in contemplative living."

Judith Couchman, author of *The Mystery of the Cross* and *The Art of Faith*

"This is a beautiful and inspiring work that will help you reflect and respond to God not just with your mind but also with your heart and soul."

Ruth Haley Barton, president, Transforming Center,
and author of *Strengthening the Soul of Your Leadership*

"This book is a unique gift for those involved in spiritual direction and biblical reflection. Juliet's delightful insights and thoughtful meditations bring the gospel stories to life. Her understanding of the artwork gives new perspectives as well as invites the reader into sacred space."

Irene Alexander, spiritual director, psychologist and educator,
Brisbane, Australia

"Where there is no vision people perish. In *Contemplative Vision* Juliet Benner enlivens us to see in the visible those things that are invisible. Her icon-mediations left me with a lingering sense of wonder, awe and reverence."

Trevor Hudson, South African pastor
and author of *Discovering Our Spiritual Identity*

"It is hard not to say 'I told you so.' The first time I read Juliet Benner's 'Oh Taste & See' column for *Conversations* journal I knew she had a rare gift for seeing—what others may miss—and describing—in a way that touches the soul—and I was pretty sure a wonderful book would follow. Here it is! A blending of biblical passages and the visual representation of the stories; lectio on contemplative steroids."

Gary W. Moon, M.Div., Ph.D., Richmont Graduate University
and author of *Apprenticeship with Jesus*

"Juliet Benner's *Contemplative Vision* is a feast! Using her impressive scholarship gently and graciously, she invites the reader to see our familiar story with new eyes. This is a book to be read slowly and savored, a book to be kept close at hand to be picked up again and again. Her suggestions and questions for reflection make it ideal as a theme for small groups or as the focus for retreats.

"A delightful and lavish feast, it left me hungry for more!"

Margaret Guenther, author of *Holy Listening* and *At Home in the World*

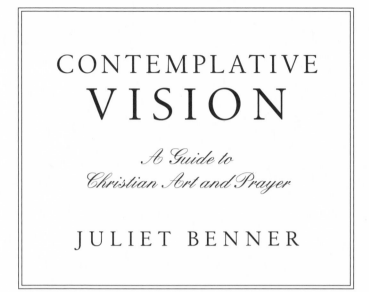

CONTEMPLATIVE
VISION

*A Guide to
Christian Art and Prayer*

JULIET BENNER

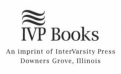

IVP Books

An imprint of InterVarsity Press
Downers Grove, Illinois

InterVarsity Press
P.O. Box 1400, Downers Grove, IL 60515-1426
World Wide Web: www.ivpress.com
E-mail: email@ivpress.com

InterVarsity Press® is the book-publishing division of InterVarsity Christian Fellowship/USA®, a movement of students and faculty active on campus at hundreds of universities, colleges and schools of nursing in the United States of America, and a member movement of the International Fellowship of Evangelical Students. For information about local and regional activities, write Public Relations Dept., InterVarsity Christian Fellowship/USA, 6400 Schroeder Rd., P.O. Box 7895, Madison, WI 53707-7895, or visit the IVCF website at <www.intervarsity.org>.

All Scripture quotations, unless otherwise indicated, are taken from the New American Standard Bible®, copyright 1960, 1962, 1963, 1968, 1971, 1972, 1973, 1975, 1977, 1995 by The Lockman Foundation. Used by permission.

The quotation from Kathy Hughes's "Love with No Edges" on page 128 is used by permission of the author.

The poem "Wounded" by John Shaw on page 97 is from A Widening Light: Poems of the Incarnation (Wheaton, Ill.: Harold Shaw, 1984). Reprinted by Regent College Publishing in 1994 and 1997. Used by permission.

Image credits and permissions are listed on page 180.

Design: Cindy Kiple

Cover image: Christ in the House of Martha and Mary, c.1654-56 (oil on canvas), Vermeer, Jan (1632-75) / © National Gallery of Scotland, Edinburgh, Scotland / The Bridgeman Art Library.

ISBN 978-0-8308-3544-7

Printed in the United States of America ∞

 InterVarsity Press is committed to protecting the environment and to the responsible use of natural resources. As a member of Green Press Initiative we use recycled paper whenever possible. To learn more about the Green Press Initiative, visit <www.greenpressinitiative.org>.

Library of Congress Cataloging-in-Publication Data

Benner, Juliet, 1946-
  Contemplative vision: a guide to Christian art and prayer / Juliet
Benner.
     p. cm.
  Includes bibliographical references (p.   ).
  ISBN 978-0-8308-3544-7 (pbk.: alk. paper)
  1. Contemplation. 2. Christian art and symbolism—Meditations. 3.
Bible—Meditations. I. Title.
  BV5091.C7B39 2010
  242'.5—dc22

                                                          2010033185

| P | 18 | 17 | 16 | 15 | 14 | 13 | 12 | 11 | 10 | 9 | 8 | 7 | 6 | 5 | 4 | 3 | 2 | 1 |
| Y | 26 | 25 | 24 | 23 | 22 | 21 | 20 | 19 | 18 | 17 | 16 | 15 | 14 | 13 | 12 | 11 |

CONTENTS

PART THREE: TRANSFORMED LIVING

To David and Sean

My two shining stars who help me see

In memory of my parents,

James and Agnes Sookhbirsingh,

who nurtured my eyes of wonder

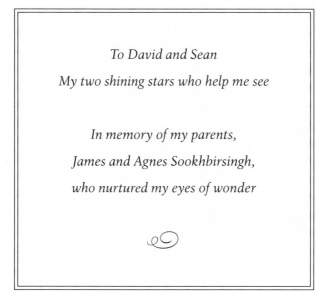

ACKNOWLEDGMENTS

*T*his book would not have been written without the encouragement and help of numerous people. The seeds were first planted in the late 1990s when I introduced art meditations to a Bible study I led at Central Presbyterian in Hamilton, Ontario. I thank Reverend Alan McPherson for his trust and for the freedom he allowed me in creating a contemplative space for our study group.

For the past fifteen years I have been leading contemplative retreats around the world. These have been rich experiences that provided much of the material for the meditations of this book. I thank especially those who have arranged these retreats as well as those who have attended and participated, offering new insights to our ways of seeing. I am particularly grateful to Pam Guneratnam and Lilian Koh Bee in Malaysia; Danny and Julie Ng in Singapore; Ekman Tam and Pui Fong Wong at Tao Fong Shan Christian Centre in Hong Kong; Jonathan and Thelma Nambu in the Philippines; Lidia Lae, Catherine Chan, Irene Alexander, and Jenny Dawson and Neil Dawson in Australia; Jerry Braun-Douglas, Ruth Penney and Kathy Hughes of the New Zealand Christian Counselling Association in New Zealand; Knut Grønvik, Janet Reidar Erikson and Bent Reidar Erikson in Norway; Inge Dahl in Denmark; Sue

Erickson, Trinity Grace Church in New York; and Gary Moon and Jeff Terrell, Richmont Graduate University in Atlanta.

Closer to home in Canada, I acknowledge with gratitude Beverley McDonald, The Sisters of Providence, Kingston, Ontario; Beth McKay Reilly, Canadian Association of Parish Nurse Ministry, Hamilton, Ontario; Cam Yates and Joan Yates, Carey Centre for Spirituality, Vancouver; Chris Houston and Jeannie Houston, Nassagaweya the Retreat, Moffat, Ontario; Sandra Broadus, Tyndale Theological College and Seminary, Toronto, Ontario; Logan McMenamie, Christ Church Cathedral, Victoria, British Columbia; and Allan Saunders, First Metropolitan United Church, Victoria, British Columbia.

So many of my friends have been faithful supporters of this project and have shared deep conversation and rich discussion, which stimulated the writing of this book. I especially thank my spiritual companions David Sigston and Bonnie Sigston, Carrie Peddle, Johanna Terbogt, Ed Plantinga and Eileen Plantinga, my spiritual director, Sr. Anne McLoughlin, S.J., Mark Muldoon, Donna McCloskey, Brenda Stephenson and Jackie Stinton.

Eternal thanks to my husband, David G. Benner, who supported my endeavor with saintly patience, encouragement and stalwart faith in me. My deep appreciation to Gary Moon for his persistent encouragement to take my articles originally written for *Conversations Journal* and develop them into a book. I also express my gratitude to my very capable editor, Cindy Bunch, for her valuable and generous input in making this a better book. And finally, my thanks to all of my family, especially my sister Cynthia for her constant reminders in times of discouragement and struggle that I had the ability to see this through to its fulfilment.

INTRODUCTION

CHRISTIAN ART AND TRANSFORMATION

ℰ

*W*hat images and inner associations come to you when you think of contemplative prayer? Perhaps what you see is a convent with nuns sitting in prayerful stillness in their room or a chapel, or possibly walking quietly by a stream. Or maybe you see a monastery with monks walking in silence through cloisters, listening to the gentle call of the abbey church bells as they move from silent personal prayer to communal prayer. But can you see yourself in the picture that forms for you? If so, what are you doing? How do you look? From that picture, what can you tell—or guess—about what might be going on in your spirit and soul?

Our ideas and images of contemplative prayer often serve as an unhelpful distraction. Too easily they suggest that this is a prayer form for spiritual elites—perhaps for those who are professionally religious. But this could not be further from the truth. Contemplative prayer is for all Christians. It is our response to God's invitation to relational intimacy.

Contemplative prayer is simply a receptive form of prayer in which we open ourselves to God in stillness and silence. It is being with God, giving the Holy Spirit the freedom to act and lead however the Spirit chooses. This involves making space for God and cultivating loving attentiveness to God. Teresa of Ávila has described it as the gaze of faith that is fixed on Jesus— sharing time alone with a good friend. While it can involve reading Scriptures, when this forms part of contemplative prayer we do not read primarily to get something or other from the passage, but simply as a way of being with God in openness and attentiveness. This openness and attentiveness is inner solitude and silence—a posture of quietly listening to God, being with God and responding to God's invitations to intimacy. Regular practice of this type of prayer is not merely a discipline but is a way of moving prayer from the closet to the rest of our life. As our relationship with God deepens, we find that every aspect of our life is touched and transformed, and we begin to see as God sees and respond as God would respond. In short, contemplative prayer is transformational because it is the way we acquire the mind, the eyes and the heart of Christ.

In his book *Divine Beauty*, John O'Donohue states, "We live between the act of awakening and the act of surrender." He goes on to argue that both awakening and surrender are shaped by seeing because *how* we see determines *what* we see, and what we see shapes the soul. This is why seeing is so foundational to the spiritual journey. When we are blind to God's presence in the midst of our lives, we are unable to see where and how God is working to transform us and the world. Surrender to God becomes a natural response when we awaken to the reality of God's love and presence that surrounds and sustains us. The more we open ourselves to God the more our clouded vision becomes clear and pure. Jesus teaches us in the Beatitudes that those who are pure in heart will see God. Purity of heart begins with purity of vision.

LEARNING TO SEE

If you do not normally think of yourself as visually challenged, you might be surprised to hear me speak of learning to see. However, I have come to think of us all as much more visually challenged than we realize. I am astounded by how poorly we actually see what is around and in front of us. I am also deeply impressed by the fact that our spiritual seeing is conditioned by our physical seeing. If we go through life oblivious to the things that our physical eyes invite us to notice, it is almost impossible for us to be truly attentive to spiritual realities.

I have long been interested in seeing. My training as a visual artist first oriented me to the priority of careful noticing. Then, working for many years as a docent in an art gallery, I found the core of my work to be teaching people how to really see what they were looking at. This translated well into my subsequent work as a spiritual director, where I found myself trying to help people learn to see God in their lives. It was here, and in retreat work, that I discovered the enormous potential of physical seeing as a doorway to spiritual seeing. I began teaching people how to read (or see) works of religious art—particularly, Judeo-Christian art that was produced as a meditation on a passage of Scripture. What I was teaching was, of course, a way of encountering the Word behind both the words of Scripture and the artist's meditation on Scripture. I was teaching, therefore, a way of using the work of art as an aid to contemplative prayer.

This is what we will be doing in this book. We will be reading biblical passages contemplatively and then looking prayerfully at visual representations of the stories—moving back and forth between the texts and the paintings. As we do so, we will be learning to pay attention—to open ourselves in trust and openness. And because we will be attending in this contemplative way to God, we will be practicing prayer.

THE ROLE OF ART IN CHRISTIAN TRADITION

Throughout history, humans have sought transcendence through embodied gods, ones they could see and touch. Their deities were represented in painted or carved images of stone or wood. In contrast, Jewish, Muslim and later Christian religious traditions forbade any visual representation of God. They considered images to be idols made by human hands, not the true and living God. Their God was communicated through their sacred Scriptures, which remained, nonetheless, rich in imagery and word pictures.

However, as evidenced by the walls of the catacombs in Rome, the earliest Christians found rich ways to express biblical stories in pictures and mosaics. In order to honor the second commandment—"You shall not make yourself an idol, or any likeness of what is in heaven"—they were careful to not depict God the Father. Following Jewish tradition, the Lord God was considered to be so holy that even to look upon him meant certain death (Exodus 33:20). However, with the birth of Christ, God acquired a human face. The Gospel of John tells us that "the Word became flesh, and dwelt among us, and we saw His glory, glory as of the only begotten from the Father, full of grace and truth" (John 1:14). When God took on flesh, the invisible became visible. Now that God could be seen, the Word-made-flesh could be expressed in image with impunity.

As Christianity spread beyond Palestine, its art became more prolific, reaching its height in the Middle Ages in Europe. Biblical art that began as expressions of the artists' own meditation on Scripture was offered as an aid to deeper understanding of faith and a resource for prayer and worship. Primarily it served as a manual for spiritual instruction. Gregory the Great expressed the power of the painted image in this age by saying that the purpose of painting is for the illiterate what writing is for those who read. Often referred to as the poor man's Bible, the value of Christian art was, however, in no way limited to the poor and the illiterate.

These great works of art were not simply *housed* in churches. Rather, they were central to the way churches proclaimed the Word. With walls and windows covered with visual depictions from the Bible in painting, stone, mosaics and stained glass, listeners to the Word could see and contemplatively engage with what they were hearing. They could personally enter into the stories and become participants in them. The Word became more real, more present.

The cathedrals themselves expressed the gospel in their architectural details. Central to their theology was the cross, which became foundational to their design and construction. It provided the footprint of the cathedral, with the long nave forming the vertical arm of the cross and the transept constituting the horizontal arm. At the meeting point of these arms worshipers received the sacrament of the Eucharist, the body and blood of Christ. Sign and symbol were as central to their worship as the visual depictions and audible readings of the Word.

Approaching the cathedral as they journeyed from home to church, medieval Christians would first see the spires, towering over everything else on the landscape and inviting them to prayer. It was a visual reminder to lift their hearts and eyes toward heaven, as well as a reminder that God was at the center of their life, at the center of their community. Moving closer to the grand edifice, they would begin to see the details of the façade. This would help prepare their hearts for worship and for receiving the holy sacrament. Approaching the massive main doors, they would see a depiction of the work of Christ in the sculptures and friezes that filled the archways leading into the sanctuary—depictions of his birth, death and resurrection, as well as the representations of the apostles and saints. The latter would remind them that they were part of a large company of believers, the "cloud of witnesses" with whom their worship was shared. Surrounded outside and inside by a wealth of rich and evocative images from the Bible, they were constantly drawn to look, to behold the glory of God and to worship with humility of heart.

Christian artists and artisans continued to make religious art uninterruptedly until the Reformation, which brought with it an emphasis on the Word. For Protestants the Word of God alone took pre-eminence, and visual images were removed from places of worship. Many of the great works of biblical art were either completely obliterated or whitewashed to cover them over. Seeing and knowing was replaced by listening and believing.

OPEN IN HEART AND MIND

Part of the cost of this movement from experiencing God through the senses and imagination to a more rational comprehension of truth was the constriction of the channels through which we access grace. God wants to meet us in heart and mind, body and soul, senses and imagination. Our experience of the divine is tremendously limited when we engage with Scriptures merely by means of intellectual understanding and belief.

Christian art provides a way of opening ourselves in our depths and totality to an encounter with God. By learning how to engage biblical stories with the totality of our being, the Word gains access to the deep places within us that cannot be reached by words or reason alone. It opens us to the mystery of that which cannot be reduced to thoughts or beliefs. It helps us love God with all of our heart, all of our mind, all of our soul and all of our strength.

From its beginnings Christianity has been a religion of seeing. Invitations such as "stand by and see the salvation of the LORD" (Exodus 14:13), "behold the beauty of the LORD" (Psalm 27:4), "Let us go . . . and see this thing that has happened" (Luke 2:15), and "O taste and see" (Psalm 34:8) draw us toward the One who is the light of the world. He was the One who would fulfill the Old Testament promise to be a lamp to our feet and a light to our path (Psalm 119:105). The shepherds and the wise men who hurried to the manger were able to see with their own eyes the King who was announced by angels and a star. Simeon, on seeing the baby Jesus in the temple, could say that his eyes had seen the fulfillment of the promise of salvation. He had seen God made flesh.

Jesus came to preach the gospel, to release captives, to bring sight to blind eyes and to proclaim God's favor. Repeatedly he invited people to have the eyes of their hearts and minds open and receptive to who he was and what he was offering. He praised those who could see: "Blessed are your eyes, because they see" (Matthew 13:16). And he rebuked those who thought they could see but were blind. In Mark 8:18 Jesus reminds his listeners of the prophet Jeremiah's rebuke: "HAVING EYES, DO YOU NOT SEE? AND HAVING EARS, DO YOU NOT HEAR?" He reserved his harshest censure for religious leaders whom he described as blind guides leading their equally blind followers toward a pit, where they eventually fall to their death (Matthew 15:14).

THE BLIND LEADING THE BLIND

Bruegel the Elder's painting of this story, *The Parable of the Blind*, is a powerful visual reminder of our need to have eyes that are clear and focused on God. Take a moment and look at the painting (see center section, or you can also find the art we will be considering on the Internet). Take your time and allow yourself to really see and experience the story it tells.

The painting depicts six sightless men walking down a slope that leads toward the village pond. One has already fallen in and lies helplessly on his back, still clutching his walking stick. The others cling to each other and to their canes, forming a strong diagonal line across the painting. The descending angle of the slope is echoed in the sticks, serving to highlight the oncoming disaster. Notice the unfocused eyes of the blind men and their downward progression as each stumbles precipitately forward, finally tumbling into the murky waters. Their faces express different responses to their plight—trust, surprise and shock. We can easily imagine how the journey ends for them. The blind men remind us of the inevitable lot of those who fail to see and respond to God's gracious presence and work in the world.

Notice the angle of the walking stick the third man carries. Allow your eyes to continue its trajectory. Then draw your attention toward the church in the background. Its tall spire prominently reaches upward toward heaven. Proverbs 4:25-26 exhorts us to let our

> eyes look directly ahead,
> And let your gaze be fixed straight in front of you.
> Watch the path of your feet
> And all your ways will be established.

The church's steeple in this painting stands as a reminder of the necessity of looking to God and to the light of the Word to illuminate our path. It is the artist's way of reminding us that if we follow Christ rather than blind guides, we will be led to eternal life and perfect peace. The painting also invites us to see truth so that we may then lead others to the One who is truth.

ART AS AN AID TO PRAYER AND LIFE

In the rest of this book we will be using biblical art as a way of opening ourselves to the Scriptures they were based on. We will be meditating on Scriptures, not simply art. We will be allowing the meditation on Scriptures, which the art represents, to lead us back to a deeper engagement with the Word.

Whenever we read or listen to the Word, we naturally and unconsciously create mental pictures of the events. This is because God gave us an imagination and intends that it, along with our mind, serve as channels through which God may touch our heart. Great Christian art helps this happen. It allows us to go beyond our own limited imagination. We are invited to participate with the artist to see and experience God in new and fresh ways. When we do so, our senses are awakened and we become more attentive and fully alive. As we prayerfully gaze on the painting, we enter the scene it depicts—into its time and place. When we do this, all time becomes present time, and we are led into the eternal presence—into the One who is ever present to us. Such openness allows us to be filled more completely with the Spirit and drawn into a deeper relationship with God.

The paintings in this book are visual expressions of biblical stories. Each painting represents the artist's personal interpretation of the story he has meditated on. Most of us are quite familiar with these stories but may need help in knowing how to read the visual symbols that artists use to tell the stories on canvas. Our "reading" of these works is, of course, a subjective process. Each of us will see different things in the paintings. In this book I offer my own interpretations and insights on each painting, but I encourage you to use them simply as a springboard to the discovery of your own.

Our focus will not be art appreciation or analysis, but using the art as an aid to prayer. Having said this, you will notice that I will make reference to some compositional details in our exploration of the paintings. I include them when they help us to enter more fully into the art and to engage more deeply with the text behind it. Remember, most of these works were created to lead the viewer into a more profound personal engagement with Scripture. The compositional structure of the art is a deliberate device by the artist to help us do that and to open our eyes to new ways of seeing. It also helps us engage with the art prayerfully. John Drury, dean of Christ Church Cathedral in Oxford, notes that viewing works of art "entails a contemplative waiting upon them which puts us alongside those who painted and viewed them so devoutly by putting us in the realm of prayer, with its passive expectancy, its active openness." He goes on to say that "worship and looking at pictures require the same kind of attention—a mixture of curiosity with a relaxed readiness to let things suggest themselves in their own good time."

This book is an invitation to such a prayer posture. It will provide you with practice in being actively open to God and passively expectant of whatever God wants to reveal to you. It is an invitation to become as a child again with a heart and mind that are open and free, and an imagination that boldly and unselfconsciously gazes at the face of the Father. It is an invitation to contemplative prayer—a prayer of self-forgetting based on a posture of total absorption in the person of God. It is an invitation to be "lost in wonder, love and praise" as we sit in stillness before God. It is an invitation to let go of all that keeps you from being fully present and open to God.

Encountering God in deeper ways often makes us want to build an altar and stay in the place of the experience. But God's call always involves an invitation to return to our lived realities. Once we experience the deeper truths of God we cannot, we dare not, remain the same. True spiritual transformation is incomplete until we live out our faith in our church communities and in the world.

Becoming attuned to the Spirit of God through the practice of contemplative prayer, we find that we also become more attuned to others. Seeing God in new and deeper ways, praying in a more receptive and open way, we then have the opportunity to respond to God and to others out of this experience. To be a contemplative, we do not need to remove ourselves from the real world. Rather, we involve ourselves fully in the center of the world and offer our prayer and service to God from there. The call is to live the Word— to put into practice the love of God, to share God's life with others. This means extending compassion and love to those whose lives touch ours. It involves helping others to become more aware of God in their life—gently drawing them into new ways of seeing and responding to God. Jesus, the light of the world, tells us that we are to be people who shed his light abroad whenever we reach out to others in love.

Allow these meditations on art and Scripture to awaken and

enliven your imagination, to nurture a closer walk with God through your contemplation, and to prompt you to respond to God with praise, wonder and worship—to "ponder anew what the Almighty can do" not only in your life but in the lives of others.

LOOKING AHEAD

But in case you are beginning to wonder if a book built around looking at art is for you, let me say something briefly about who I have had in mind as I have written this book. My target audience is Christians who want to know God more deeply. Lots of books tell you about God. This book has been designed to lead you toward a *personal* knowing of God—the sort of knowing that can only come from time spent with God in stillness. This inner stillness and attentiveness is, as I have said, contemplative prayer. Attending to art will be the means to that end, not the end. You don't even have to like art to benefit from this book. Many people who have come to retreats or lectures I have offered on this topic have told me that they have never gone to art galleries or had any interest in art. They did, however, want to learn to be with God in stillness and attentiveness. That is the longing that the Spirit of God can satisfy when we take time to sit in contemplative stillness before the Word of God and before art that has been produced as a meditation on it.

The book is organized into three sections, taking us on a progressive journey from awakening to God through learning how to see and finally to transformed living. Part one will consider the ways we fail to see God in our daily life and how we can grow in our awareness of God. In part two we will practice contemplative seeing and notice how this moves us toward a transformed vision. Finally, we will examine how transformed vision will shape the way we live in and relate to the world. Here we will explore the possibilities of deeper living in the fullness of the Spirit that is possible because we have learned to see with God's eyes and respond with God's heart of love and compassion.

As you read this book, keep in mind the following suggestions.

This book is best read slowly and contemplatively. Don't read it in order to grasp content. Read it to allow God to grasp you. Don't rush to finish a chapter or a section. This is a prayer process and should not be hurried. Linger wherever God is meeting you, and receive whatever is there for you as a gift. While there is a logical flow to the chapters, it is not necessary to read them in consecutive order. If you prefer, allow yourself to be led by interest, choosing chapters whose titles resonate with your spirit. All you need is a heart and mind that is open and receptive to whatever God wants for you. Come with no agenda other than to meet God and to give yourself over to the Spirit's guidance.

Make your reading and contemplation an act of prayer. Begin by sitting in a quiet place where you can comfortably open yourself to God. If you find it helpful, you may want to include a visual reminder of the presence of the Spirit with a lit candle or something personally meaningful for you. Take a moment to be silently present to God. Ask for the guidance of the Holy Spirit to see and hear what God wants you to see and hear. And thank God for being present with you, in Word and Spirit.

Read the biblical text slowly. Most of the chapters in this book are built around a biblical text and a painting that has been produced as a meditation on that text. You will encounter the text early in each chapter. Read this passage—which is usually quite short—slowly and contemplatively. You might want to read it several times, possibly from different translations. Do not look for insights or try to analyze the passage. Simply allow it to wash over you. Listen with your heart and pay attention to any words or phrases that catch your attention. Notice what sensations, memories and associations come to you—in your body, mind, heart or emotions. Stay with these, allowing the Spirit to use them to draw you closer to God.

Then turn your attention to the painting that corresponds

to the passage. If you have access to a computer, you might want to download an Internet version of the art for a more detailed viewing. Sometimes it helps to use a magnifying glass to see the details better. But whether you examine it on the pages at the center of the book or on a computer screen, take a long, slow look at the painting. Look at the way it supports the text and the word or phrase you have been holding. Notice how your perception changes or remains the same as you pay attention to its details. And as you read the rest of the chapter, allow it to help you enter into the painting and thereby deepen your engagement with the text.

Each chapter will conclude with questions for reflection. The questions are intended to provide you with an opportunity for deeper engagement with both the paintings and the biblical texts they are based on. Use them as a way of noticing and responding to the gifts and invitations that you may have received from the Spirit of God. Consider responding to each chapter with your own creative expression. Perhaps you might want to paint or draw your own interpretation of the story, or write a poem or a piece of music, or express yourself in some other way. But do respond. And do thank God for the new ways of seeing that are becoming yours—and for the growing awareness of God's closeness to you that I pray you will experience.

Appendix one offers some suggestions as to how to use this book if you are leading a group that is discussing it as a framework for contemplative prayer. Appendix two addresses spiritual directors and offers suggestions about how the book can be used in their work, as well as some more general comments on the way they can employ contemplation on religious art in their spiritual companioning.

All of this I offer with the prayer that God will use these meditations to infuse your spirit with the Spirit of Christ and deepen your awareness of God's love for you. May you be drawn closer to the heart of God. And may you be graced with transformed vision as a route to a transformed life as God's love flows through you to others.

FOR REFLECTION AND DISCUSSION

- Take a moment to sit in quietness and openness before God. Reflect on the ways God has been present in your life over the years, even during times when you were not attentive to such presence. How has God been present to you in recent days? How do you notice God's presence? And how do you respond to it?

- How do you react to the invitation of this chapter to live more attentive to the presence of God? What would change in your life if you were to encounter God as a little child? How do you choose to respond to the invitation of Jesus to become like a little child?

- Think for a moment about the John Drury quotes I shared in this chapter. He described the contemplative viewing of art that we will be doing together as prayer because of its passive expectancy and active openness toward God. How important does this posture seem to you? What things keep you from such a contemplative posture of attentive openness? Drury suggests that contemplation involves a mixture of curiosity and a relaxed readiness to let things suggest themselves in their own good time. How might this apply to waiting for God in stillness in your life?

Part One

TRANSFORMED AWARENESS

AWAKENING

Bruegel the Elder
Census at Bethlehem

or many of us, the invitation to contemplative stillness before God is both appealing and slightly threatening. It suggests a way of being that might seem desirable but probably feels alien. If we are honest, we have to admit that there is very little stillness in our spirits. We go through week after week, month after month, preoccupied with the business of daily life—our jobs (sometimes finding one and at other times keeping on top of the one we have), maintaining a home and family, perhaps struggling to keep afloat in hard economic times. We are so used to being busy that we treat it as an essential characteristic of the good life. Ask people how they are doing and they will often answer by telling you how busy they are. It has become a mark of success—as if someone who is not busy must certainly be leading an unfulfilling and unsuccessful life. If we are busy, we feel that life is meaningful.

Human beings have become human doings. Simply being feels like not enough—perhaps even personal failure. We have failed to nurture solitude and stillness of heart, both of which are at the heart of prayer. Contemplative living just does not seem realistic in our busy lives and worlds.

But our problem is deeper than busyness. Tragically, we live much of our lives on automatic pilot. We go through our days as sleep walkers—unaware of God's presence, inattentive to God's gifts and invitations, and failing to be present to either ourselves or God. We fail to notice that God is in the ordinary events of our ordinary days. God is present—in the world around us, in the people whom we encounter and in our work. Sadly, it is we who are absent.

How can we hope to be attentive to the presence of God when we can't even see the ordinary things before our eyes as we move through our day? In our frenzied world we so easily miss the fragrance of a flower, the beauty of trees in new growth, or of the aroma of fresh bread wafting from a bakery as we rush by. We are barely conscious of the music of birdsong, of a gentle wind as it brushes our cheek and hair, of the gurgling of stream or fountain. We fail to attend to the taste of rain on our lips as we run for shelter or of snowflakes gently falling on our faces. The list goes on and on. All of our senses have become dulled as we live life in a state of preoccupation and distraction. Yet God is always present in our lives whether we notice or not. C. S. Lewis reminds us that "we may ignore, but we can nowhere evade the presence of God. The world is crowded with Him. He walks everywhere *incognito*. And the *incognito* is not always hard to penetrate. The real labour is to remember, to attend. In fact, to come awake. Still more, to remain awake."

Contemplative prayer is awakening and attentiveness. It is stepping back from our preoccupations and distractions and allowing God to transform our awareness, our hearts and our lives. It is making space to be with God in stillness and solitude. It is not withdrawing from the world to go into the desert or monastery to find undisturbed serenity and peace. It is allowing the Spirit to cultivate an inner stillness of heart that persists even in the busyness and challenges of our lives, and that allows us to face those

challenges with focus and passion that comes from living with at-
tunement to God.

But, you might ask, how can we develop such a posture of heart?
It starts with practicing attentiveness in the ordinary course of life.
It begins with consciously making space for the present moment
and for life as it is. If we are not present to the now, we can never
be present to the God who was revealed to Moses as "I AM"—the
eternal One who is with us in the present moment. We can remember how God has met us in the past and we can wait with hope for
how we trust God will meet us in the future, but we can only actually meet God in the present moment.

OPENING OUR EYES—LOOKING

Stop for a moment and look at the second painting (see center
section).* It is another by the same artist we encountered in the
introduction—Bruegel the Elder. Take time to look at it carefully
and contemplatively. What do you see?

Perhaps you noticed all the busyness—a crowded village scene
filled with peasants going about their daily activities. On the left of
the painting we see a throng of people gathered in front of a building, while others nearby are working at their different tasks—
woodworking, slaughtering pigs, carrying wood. All around there
is action and purposeful movement. People bearing heavy loads
walk carefully across the icy lake. Some are constructing a building in the upper right. A woman brushes away snow with her
broom. Children play on the ice, and some toss snowballs at each
other. Bruegel includes new and old buildings, some large and sub-
stantial—the tall, sturdy church (look far back in the upper left
corner of the painting)—and some falling into ruin (on the opposite side of the canvas). There are carts laden with kindling and
kegs of water or wine. This is life at its most ordinary—people

---

*On the Internet go to <http://d1shzm2uca9f83.cloudfront.net/large/volkstelling_
jeruzalem.jpg>.

Bruegel the Elder (1525-1569)

The exact details of Bruegel's life are uncertain, but we do know that he spent most of it in Antwerp, Brussels, although he did live in Italy for a while and was greatly influenced by the Italian Renaissance style. While he spent most of his life in cities, he was best known for his paintings of landscapes and country life. He enjoyed dressing up as a peasant in order to mingle with the common folk in order to draw inspiration and authentic details for his paintings. This earned him the nickname of Peasant Bruegel. Many of his everyday scenes are filled with subtle commentaries on the religious controversies of his time. His faith provided many of the themes for his religious works.

The painting *The Parable of the Blind* (1568) hangs in the National Museum of Capodimonte in Naples, Italy.

busy with everyday activities in a frozen, wintry landscape, as we watch the sun sinking slowly below the horizon.

But who are these people in the painting failing to see in their midst? Who, possibly, did you fail to see in their midst? The easily overlooked, central figures of the painting are Mary and Joseph. Do you see them? If not, look for the woman on the donkey in the lower center of the painting. Contextualized within a northern European landscape for Flemish viewers, the painting depicts Mary and Joseph approaching the inn to which they had traveled in order to be registered for the census. It took me a long time to find Mary and Joseph when I first looked at this painting, but once I recognized them, I was deeply moved by the fact that Jesus' presence is so often hidden from us. I realized how blind I am to his invisible presence in the midst of my busy life, and felt a longing to recognize him more often.

The painting *Census at Bethlehem* (1566) is based on Luke 2:4-5. Read the passage slowly, entering into the experience of Mary and Joseph as they make their arduous journey to Bethlehem. Pay attention to what captures your heart and mind. Then as you look at the painting, allow yourself to be drawn into the scene. Be a part of the village activities, and notice what details come to the fore.

> Joseph also went up from Galilee, from the city of Nazareth, to Judea, to the city of David which is called Bethlehem, because he was of the house and family of David, in order to register along with Mary, who was engaged to him, and was with child.

As Mary and Joseph approach the inn, the crowd ahead of them is already busily involved in this registration process. They are all absorbed in their own affairs and activities. The holy family are lost in the scene. They are right in the middle of things, but everyone is too engrossed in their preoccupations to notice them.

Bruegel has used a biblical subject to provide a realistic commentary on his own period in history. Set in his time and place, he depicts Mary and Joseph making their journey to Bethlehem to pay their taxes. It is a landscape filled with the severe reality of humanity with all its laborious toils, burdens and suffering. They are shown struggling under weighty loads, dressed in simple, rough, homespun clothing. A leper's hut (just to the right and behind the donkey) marked with a tiny cross on its crude roof and surrounded by cross-marked graves gives raw evidence of the physical challenges they face. They line up to pay their taxes too, but instead of taxes to Caesar they are weighed down under the taxes of Philip II and pay tribute to him. These cold, shivering human beings, burdened with a harsh life and eking out a living to pay their duties to their king, must have questioned the meaning of life. Yet Christ is here in their very midst, hidden and unseen. More than a commentary on Bruegel's times, it represents our own modern world. We share the same struggles and burdens, and Christ comes to us in the midst of them to share our humanity. Christ is present if only we would see him.

This painting is found in the Royal Museum of Fine Arts in Belgium. Without knowing the title you may not have realized that the theme was a religious one. But Bruegel gives us other clues to the spiritual significance of what we are viewing. The artist reputedly liked to include subtle hints of the spiritual in his paintings. Look, for example, at the large round wreath above the door of the inn. You might include evergreen wreaths among your Christmas decorations, but are you aware of their symbolic meaning? It and other circles scattered throughout the work—did you notice the numerous wagon wheels?—are symbols of eternity. Bruegel used them as ways of reminding us of the eternal significance of seeing and knowing the Christ who is in our midst.

There are other references to the life of Jesus in the painting. The ruined building in the far upper right reminds us that with the birth of Jesus, a new covenant is replacing the old. The old order is shown to be inadequate and falling into ruin. In the lower left corner we see three chickens pecking at their food in the snow. Perhaps Bruegel is referencing Peter's threefold denial during Christ's trial when the cock's crow reminded him of Jesus' words. They may point to Christ's trial and death, and the redemptive power of his crucifixion. Huge logs to the left of the chickens remind us of Jesus' own future occupation as a carpenter, with the beams resembling the cross from which he would be hung. The wagon with the kindling recalls for us the Old Testament prefiguring of Christ in Isaac's sacrifice. The wine kegs may allude to what Jesus was to call "the new covenant in my blood."

This is more than humdrum, routine existence. This is undeniably a life and world filled with the glory of God. God is indeed incognito, hidden from us but close to us and at the very heart of our life. We can begin to see God more clearly when we pay closer attention to small, seemingly insignificant signs of his presence. Bruegel's painting is an invitation for us to open our eyes, to awaken and see the Christ who is Immanuel—God with us in the very midst of our own lives, not just in this Flemish village scene.

AWARE AND AWAKE—RESPONDING

Being aware and awake is at the core of the spiritual life. We are blind and we need to learn to see. The French author Muriel Barbery reminds us of our inability to really see. Speaking through the mouth of one her characters, she tells us that "our eyes may perceive, yet they do not observe; they may believe, yet they do not question; they may receive, yet they do not search; they are emptied of desire, with neither hunger nor passion." Our sense of seeing has become empty and passionless as we look but don't really see into the depth of things. Spirituality is about seeing and about being awake. Jesus often taught about the importance of being watchful (e.g., Matthew 25:13; Luke 12:37). He taught that when our spiritual eyes are healthy and discerning, our whole body is full of light (Luke 11:34). He presents children as models of the sort of seeing that he encouraged. When he invites us to become like them, he invites us to have eyes that are free of the obstacles that blur our vision of the divine. So important is this that he stated that anyone who does not receive the kingdom of God like a child will never enter it (Luke 18:17).

Think of the way children see. Picture the total absorption of a little child as she lies on her stomach, nose pressed to the ground, her attention riveted on a tiny worm inching its way across the floor. She is oblivious to everything else around her. Her abandonment is unself-conscious and unforced, and her rapture complete. This is the kind of gazing that art invites. This gazing is, as we shall see, contemplative prayer.

Gerald Manley Hopkins begins his poem "God's Grandeur" by

saying: "The world is charged with the glory of God." He spoke what he knew, not simply what he believed. Christians affirm his theology but often share little of his spiritual experience and knowing. We go through life as sleep walkers with very limited seeing and, consequently, very limited knowing of the unseen spiritual realities. We confuse believing with experiencing. We may believe that God is present in all of life, but we do not experience this. Most of us no longer have eyes for God. Like the blind men of the first painting we looked at, we are blind to the grandeur that charges the world and unaware of God's constant presence in our midst.

If we are blind to God's presence, how can we really know God's love? Learning to really see and nurturing the art of truly seeing can be a transforming experience for us. Sight that is more than just physical, which sees beyond the material world to hidden spiritual realities, has the power to change us. Meditation on biblical art helps us regain this lost art of seeing—physically and spiritually—the presence of God in all of life. It provides practice in awareness and attentiveness to God's frequent interruptions in our daily existence. It is an aid to develop openness and receptivity to the good gifts God wants to give us. It enfleshes the gospel and helps us draw closer to God so that we live our lives for God and for others. Be alert to God's presence and action in the midst of your life. Watch constantly for God in all of life and respond to God's subtle interruptions to draw you into closer relationship.

FOR REFLECTION AND DISCUSSION

- Reread Luke 2:1-5 and look again at Breugel's *Census at Bethlehem*. Imaginatively place yourself in the painting. Where would you be and what would you be doing? What activities might keep you distracted or preoccupied, making it hard for you to notice the presence of the hidden Christ in your midst? What things in your life in recent days have kept you preoccupied and left you asleep and unaware?

- Many of the people in the painting carry heavy burdens. They are stooped under their heavy loads. What burdens do you carry that are distracting you from seeing God's presence? How do you respond to Jesus' invitation to come to him to find rest for your weary soul? Where might Christ be in the midst of your burden-carrying at the present moment?

- In this chapter I suggest that contemplative prayer involves awakening and attentiveness. It is stepping back from our preoccupations and distractions and allowing God to transform our awareness, our hearts and our lives. It starts with awakening. What things lull you back to sleep after moments of awakening? How do you choose to respond to any invitation you may be hearing from the Spirit of God to a life of deeper awareness of God's presence and the transformation of your heart and life that would flow from that?

- As a way to begin practicing awareness, consider starting with something as simple as pausing long enough to notice the texture of the food the next time you eat. When you eat, just eat. Simply be present in the moment. Offer your attentiveness in that moment as a prayer. Notice the feel of the clothes you are presently wearing. Pay attention to any smells, sounds or sensations that may be part of your experience at the moment—the smell of salty sea air, the sound of a humming air conditioner, the aftertaste of your last sip of coffee. Awareness of anything can be a doorway to awareness of God's presence. Awareness of nothing beyond your preoccupations means an inevitable lack of awareness of God's presence. Make a point of practicing awareness in the present moment and prayerfully ask God to help you discern God's presence in the moments of this day, this week and this upcoming month.

2

COMING ASIDE

MORETTO DA BRESCIA
Christ in the Wilderness

*O*ne important way of learning to be awake to the presence of God in the midst of life is to make regular time for quiet prayer and reflection. Periodic retreats from the world where we intentionally lay aside our preoccupations to be attentive to God in stillness allow God to open our eyes and develop greater awareness of God's loving presence. They are opportunities to learn to see the signs of transcendence that surround us.

SPIRITUAL RETREAT

This increased awareness of and attentiveness to God is the goal of a spiritual retreat. But before we consider what is involved in a retreat organized for this purpose, we should take a moment to be aware of how different such a retreat is from the many other activities that are confusingly also called retreats. When you think of retreat you may, for example, be thinking of a church retreat that is based primarily on fun, fellowship and teaching. Or if you are in a work context where teams periodically take retreats together, perhaps you are thinking of a time of brainstorming, reviewing and planning. Neither of these things has much in common with the classical Christian spiritual retreat.

A spiritual retreat is never simply a matter of rest or relaxation, planning or even teaching. Its focus is relational. It is centered on encountering God. A spiritual retreat is a time to set aside all our agendas, attachments and preoccupations and place ourselves completely in the hands of God. It is a response to an invitation from our heavenly Father to come away with him. God is the host of this encounter and must be, therefore, in control of the agenda. Thomas Green calls it a vacation with the Lord. Approach this vacation ready to listen for and to wait on God. This vacation isn't primarily about learning from God, but simply being with God. Do not, therefore, think of it as a time to get something done, but rather a time for God to do something in and with you.

Getting away is a central feature of a spiritual retreat. Sometimes, of course, this is impossible, and we can certainly work out some kind of a compromise retreat in a back yard or quiet room of our own house. But a degree of solitude and quietness has always been a part of how people have approached spiritual retreats, something that reaches right back to the earliest days of Christianity. In the third and fourth centuries a common pattern was to go to the deserts of Syria and Egypt, where early Christians would often meet with spiritual directors known as the desert mothers and fathers. Jesus, too, regularly practiced this sort of getting away to meet God and himself in a deeper place than was possible in the midst of daily life, and he encouraged his disciples to do the same.

The vacation retreats that God plans for us will often involve surprises, and these may not always be pleasant. Retreats are places where we are exposed to the full light of God—places where we cannot hide from God or from ourselves. The silence that comes with solitude opens up places within us where we may be led to mountains of rapture and mystical encounters, or to dark valleys where our heart is laid bare and raw before God. We may be confronted by trials and struggle as well as by joy and praise. We do not choose how God will meet us while we are alone with God in retreat, but we can rest in God's love and surrender ourselves to the gifts God provides, whether they are painful struggles or moments of ecstatic blessing.

JESUS' WILDERNESS RETREAT—LISTENING

The Gospels tell us that Jesus regularly found time to go away to lonely and isolated places for times of retreat with his Father. Although his short life was crammed with persistent pleas for healing and crushing crowds wanting to touch and hear him, Jesus always managed to find time to be alone with his Father. Jesus knew that these times were utterly essential if he was to accomplish his Father's will.

The Italian artist Moretto da Brescia presents us with his interpretation of Jesus' first recorded retreat. It comes, according to Mark, immediately after he has been baptized, just as he is about to be launched into his earthly ministry. It was an experience that we commonly describe as his temptation by the devil, and so we may not think of it as a retreat. But remember that God controls the agenda of spiritual retreats. And this was the Father's agenda for this first recorded retreat of Jesus. We too can learn much from it, for our retreats may also involve temptation, trials and an encounter with darkness—both our inner darkness and the darkness that is in the world.

We are told in the Gospel that this desert retreat of Jesus was initiated—in fact, literally "impelled"—by the Spirit. There was no question that this was the retreat of God's choosing. Take a few moments for a slow reading of the account of it presented in Mark 1:12-13. You may also find it helpful to read the corresponding accounts recorded in Matthew 4:1-11 and Luke 4:1-13 for more details. Then look carefully and meditatively at Moretto da Brescia's painting *Christ in the Wilderness*. Note the things that strike you

Moretto da Brescia (1498-1554)

Born in Brescia, Italy, as Alessandro Bonvicino and known as "Il Moretto," Moretto da Brescia learned his art as apprentice to the great Titian. He was an astute follower of the Venetian school of artists and his works reflect their influence. He was considered to be a person of great personal piety and known to prepare himself by prayer and fasting whenever he set out to produce any sacred art. His prolific *oeuvres* of altarpieces and other religious works attest to his Christian devotion and faith. He became the leading painter of his day in his city of Brescia, from where most of his art was produced.

Christ in the Wilderness was painted in 1540 and is now part of the collection of the Metropolitan Museum of Art, New York.

most forcibly. What do you see? What do you experience?

In those days Jesus came from Nazareth in Galilee and was baptized by John in the Jordan.

Immediately coming up out of the water, He saw the heavens opening, and the Spirit like a dove descending upon Him;

and a voice came out of the heavens: "You are My beloved Son, in You I am well-pleased."

Immediately the Spirit impelled Him to go out into the wilderness.

And He was in the wilderness forty days being tempted by Satan; and He was with the wild beasts, and the angels were ministering to Him. (Mark 1:9-13)

BEING WITH JESUS IN THE DESERT—LOOKING

Moretto da Brescia's desert is not a wide, sandy expanse of dunes.*
It is a place of rugged rocks punctuated by shadowed clefts with
two trees growing in the center of the painting. The tree on the left
looks dead with dry, leafless branches. The one on the right leans
toward Jesus and is alive with fresh green leaves, some on its lower
branches turning red. Unlike the dead tree, this may remind us of
the life, growth, strength and security we and Jesus have when
rooted and grounded in God's love. The left tree presents the alter-
native to this—death.

Notice the variety of animals that surround Jesus as he sits alone
on a rock. Many are creatures of the desert, the "wild beasts" of
Mark's detail in verse 13—a snake, a scorpion and a mythological
bird at Jesus' feet, ready to pounce. You have to really strain your
eyes to see the snake, his head strategically placed near Jesus' right
heel. It brings to mind God's word to the serpent in the Garden of
Eden that his head would be bruised by the descendent of Eve.
There are several types of birds, the white one atop the rock on the
left reminding us of the dove with outstretched wings that rested
over Jesus' head at his baptism. This may be the artist's way of reminding us of the Spirit's role in both his baptism and in bringing
him on this retreat. A black eagle sits atop the tallest rock also
bowed and perhaps pecking at something on the rock face. Biblical
references to eagles often convey connotations of strength and
keen insight.

Other creatures include a bear and a lion who lie meekly asleep
beside Jesus, a fox, and a stag on the left. The stag reminds us of the
psalmist's expression that his soul thirsts and searches for God as a
hart longs for a running stream. Considered to be immune to snake
venom because they drank a great deal of spring water, stags were a
symbol in medieval art of resistance to sin. All these animals seem

---

*On the Internet go to <www.metmuseum.org/toah/images/h2/h2_11.53.jpg>.

to look toward Jesus in postures of worshipful attention. Although the end of the story is not depicted here, the artist is perhaps suggesting that if we keep our focus on Jesus, the One who gives us living water, we also will be able to resist temptation.

Jesus, with a faint halo surrounding his head, sits with his cheek supported by his right hand, traditionally symbolic in art of solitary meditation. His left hand rests on his knee and one foot is placed comfortably on a small rock. He seems very still, but we also get a sense of intense inner focus and concentration. At this moment in time, the painting depicts Jesus completely centered. He does not allow any of the animals and activities that surround him to distract him. We see no disordered attachments here as Jesus prepares himself with prayer and fasting. The desert is a place where both body and soul can be severely tested and purified. Remember that Jesus was fasting for the forty days he was there. But the moment where we encounter him in this painting is before the ravages of this hunger and thirst. He has not yet been thrust into the arena of struggle with the devil.

Notice the angels that appear in the sky on both sides of the painting. They reinforce the medieval belief that our universe, the world close to us, around and above us, is inhabited by heavenly beings. They were thought to be ever present, though unseen. The ones closest to Jesus hover over him and appear to be waiting until his ordeal is over to minister to him. They seem solid and real in contrast to the more ethereal, somewhat sketchy cherubs on the left side.

None of us would voluntarily choose this kind of encounter with darkness as a retreat for ourselves. But it may be the retreat God chooses for us. In such a retreat we discover that our true home is found in the heart of God's love. Spending time soaking in God's love, we find that our real work, our vocation is made clearer. We discover that we are enabled to go out into the world with the confidence and trust that our heart is aligned with the heart of

God. This was certainly the case for Jesus as he wrestled with Satan in the desert in preparation by the Spirit for his vocation. And so it often is for us.

WAYS OF COMING ASIDE—RESPONDING

Spiritual retreats can—and do—take many different forms. Some are directed (involving daily meetings with a spiritual companion or director) while others are not. Some are solitary, while others are with a group. Some are conducted in silence, while others allow for conversation. Some involve going to a retreat center or monastery, while others happen in a log cabin in the forest, a hotel room or even a backyard.

My first retreat involved going by myself to a Canadian alpine ski lodge for a week one summer. The setting was wonderful, with lots of hiking trails, and because it was off-season there were very few people around. I simply went away for a time of solitude with God, taking along my Bible, my journal and my prayerful openness. My focus on this retreat was to set aside time for a deeper knowing of myself and God. I began every morning with a passage of Scripture—Psalm 139 was one such passage which held more than enough depth and richness for my entire week. I would then go for long, contemplative walks in the nearby forest trails and pray with the verse or text that really spoke to me. These times were powerful because they were silent times when I could listen to God's communication of love for me. They were times too when I began to see my own heart as God sees it and my need to align myself more with God's heart. Later in the day I would record in my journal what I heard or sensed of God's presence or absence through my day. I used the rest of my day expressing my response to God through music, sketching, painting or writing poetry that bubbled to the surface from my conscious prayer times. My entire week was a period of time where I simply hung out with God, waiting on and listening for God. The impact of that encounter with

God was immense, including moving me toward training in spiritual direction and the work I now do as a retreat leader.

But while you do not have to go to a desert or even to a retreat house to allow the Lord to awaken your spirit and sharpen your attentiveness to the presence and leading of the Spirit, retreats in settings dedicated to that purpose do offer significant advantages. One is that they allow you the option of the accompaniment of a spiritual companion who can assist you in being prayerfully attentive to the gifts and invitations of God. A directed retreat is not someone telling you what to do but a retreat that includes the presence of a spiritual companion who meets with you for prayer and reflection on where God is in your experience and how you are responding. But nondirected retreats can also be accommodated in most retreat houses and still offer you the blessing of knowing that those who serve you as hosts of the center are praying for you and your encounter with God. That, after all, is why they are there and are doing what they are doing.

There are as many ways of pausing from your regular life to attend to God as there are people and regular lives. I know people who feel they do not have the luxury of even a day of such solitude who have found a way to make space for just a single hour of stillness and attentiveness to God. Or, if you already take some time to read Scriptures or pray to God most days, consider making this your retreat. Perhaps the invitation the Spirit may be offering is to leave more space in it for attentiveness, making it less a time of doing and talking, and more one of listening and being with God in stillness.

Times of spiritual retreat are not opportunities to get away from the realities of our lives but times of training in awareness, attentiveness and responsiveness to God in the midst of those realities. They should prepare us to return to our regular lives with God's heart of compassion and love for ourselves, others and our world. In retreat we accept the invitation of our Lord to step back from the preoccupations and demands of daily life just long enough to restore our focus and prepare us to return to it. The same is true for viewing a work of art. To gain a better perspective and focus we have to move away from it and look at it from a distance. Nothing changes within the painting itself, but we see differently from having stepped back for a different point of view. After meeting God in retreat, the world we encounter on return will usually be composed of the same realities that were there when we left. But we will be changed and will have fresh eyes to see life more clearly. We are now newly attuned to God and aligned with God's Spirit in us and in the world.

This wilderness retreat of Jesus was a time of preparation and equipping for the ministry that lay ahead. Most important, it was a time of attentiveness to the loving presence of the one he called Father. As he ended his retreat, his focus was clear and his identity as the beloved Son more firmly established. Through this his heart and will were aligned with the heart and will of his Father, and he returned to his world with renewed focus and passion for his mission.

May this be your experience. It will be if it is indeed God's retreat, not simply yours. It will be if you allow the retreat to be used by God to open your eyes, heal your awareness, touch your heart, and awaken and realign your spirit.

FOR REFLECTION AND DISCUSSION

- Turn again to Moretto da Brescia's painting *Christ in the Wilderness*. What is your focus as you look at it? Allow yourself to be one of the animals in the painting, offering to Jesus your worship through attentive gazing. Take some time now to simply be with God in attentive stillness as you meditate on his wilderness retreat. Reread the Gospel accounts of this retreat to help you enter Jesus' retreat experience (Matthew 4:1-11; Mark

1:12-13; Luke 4:1-13). Allow the story to awaken your senses and imagination and serve as a means of grace to allow you to be with Jesus.

- Have you ever had a retreat experience that was in any way like this one of Jesus? In the midst of the desert, the living tree in the painting seems to give shade and protection to Jesus. How have you experienced such protection on occasions of retreat that were dark, unpleasant or unwelcome—not the sort of retreat you would have planned for yourself? Like this tree, where did you find growth and life?

- Sometimes when we are open to God in stillness and solitude, we are confronted with dark parts of ourselves, which can be hard to face. Sometimes we encounter "wild beasts" that turn up uninvited. Some times we encounter unwelcome temptations. What "beasts" have turned up on your retreats? How were they, or could they have been, tamed if you turned your attention to the presence of God in attentive openness and did not allow them to distract you?

- Retreats are thin places where we encounter the divine. They are places where we often hear the "rumor of angels." Has this ever been your experience on a retreat? If so, how have you felt ministered to by God's attendants?

- After reading this chapter, pay attention to any invitation you may experience from the Spirit to come aside and be still with God? If this is your experience, how do you choose to respond? Don't allow your response to simply be your creation of the retreat you think you need or want. Allow it to be a response to the Lord's invitation to the retreat that God invites you to right now.

3

GAZING IN STILLNESS

JOHANNES VERMEER
Jesus in the House of Mary and Martha

⁓

*I*nner stillness is essential for spiritual attentiveness but it is the means, not the end. Contemplative prayer is not a strategy for stress management or a form of relaxation. Because it is prayer, it involves a relationship. It is being with and being drawn closer to God.

The goal of contemplative prayer is not to try and make yourself still. This is both impossible and misses the point that prayer is an encounter with God, not a spiritual self-improvement technique or a stress-management strategy. The goal of stillness before God is to be totally open to God and, in the words of Cynthia Bourgeault, to "consent to the presence and action of God within us in whatever form it comes." The purpose of the stillness is to enable us to attend to God and to be fully and without distraction with God. It is to know God in the way that is only possible in stillness. Recall the remarkable words of Psalm 46:10—"Be still, and know that I am God" (NIV). Stillness is a form of spiritual perception. In stillness we can encounter God, and God us, in ways that are impossible under any other conditions.

In the painting we considered in the last chapter we saw Jesus sitting in utter absorption in the desert. We saw him in contemplative stillness, oblivious to the distractions around him and uniquely open to and in touch with the Father. Looking on, we were able to be a witness to the intimate encounter with his Father that this moment represented. It was a moment of intense prayer. Silence and stillness were the means by which the inexpressible in his heart were communicated by the Spirit to the Father.

Silence and stillness offer us the same opportunity for intimate encounter with God. In stillness we can hear God's word. Contemplation on works of art that are created as meditations on Scriptures may superficially appear to be the external focus of our attention, but in reality, if we are seeking God, they are not simply an aesthetic experience; as we sit before them in prayer they become a means to open ourselves to God. They are not the object of prayer, but an aid to prayer. Stillness and attentiveness are the means through which symbols speak their meaning to mind and spirit, and God's Word is spoken into our hearts.

JESUS IN THE HOUSE OF
MARY AND MARTHA—LISTENING

Mary, the sister of Martha and Lazarus, is often rightly identified as a woman who knew how to live life in this deep place of stillness and openness to God. While it is unlikely that she ever attended a workshop on contemplative prayer or read any books or articles on the topic, she lived in a posture that is captured in the next piece of art I want us to consider. The painting is by the Dutch artist Vermeer and is his artistic response to a meditation on Luke 10:38-42.

Now as they were traveling along, He entered a village; and a woman named Martha welcomed Him into her home.

She had a sister called Mary, who was seated at the Lord's feet, listening to His word.

But Martha was distracted with all her preparations; and she came up to Him and said, "Lord, do You not care that my sister has left me to do all the serving alone? Then tell her to help me."

But the Lord answered and said to her, "Martha, Martha, you are worried and bothered about so many things;

but only one thing is necessary, for Mary has chosen the good part, which shall not be taken away from her."

This passage is the account of Jesus' visit to the home of Mary and Martha. Vermeer's focus is verse 39: "Mary . . . was seated at the Lord's feet, listening to His word." As we look at his painting we

---

Johannes Vermeer (1632-1675)

Born in Delft, Johannes Vermeer was a Dutch artist who was not recognized for his art until only a hundred years ago. He has come to our most recent notice through the movie based on the novel by Tracy Chevalier, *Girl with the Pearl Earring*— the title of book and movie based on a visually stunning painting by Vermeer with the same title.

Jesus in the House of Mary and Martha (1654) was one of Vermeer's earliest paintings and his only known religious work. Raised in a Reformed Protestant home, Vermeer would have been immersed in the stories of the Bible and would have known this particular Gospel account well. He later converted to Catholicism when he married Catharina Bolnes, who bore him fifteen children. His father was a weaver of fine fabrics as well as an art dealer and innkeeper. Many of Vermeer's paintings give evidence of his exposure to color and texture of fabrics from his close proximity to his father's business.

pray that we may be guided into stillness before the text that the Spirit may then use to allow us to hear the Word behind the words.

Before looking at the painting, take time for a slow meditative reading of this story of Jesus' visit with the two sisters. Read it as if for the first time. Notice any new images or thoughts that come to your mind. Notice the picture of the scene that emerges in your own mind. After you have done this, spend time looking at the painting (see back cover). Sit quietly and comfortably, without any distractions, and prayerfully seek the guidance of the Holy Spirit—asking for your eyes and heart to be opened to the spiritual realities that it presents.

FIRST IMPRESSIONS—LOOKING

Vermeer's rendering of this well-known story depicts the three friends together in a room.* It shows the moment where Jesus responds to Martha's complaint about Mary's apparent neglect in helping her.

How does this painting change or enhance your understanding of the story? What is your initial response to it? How is this scene different from the one you may have formed in your imagination as you read the story?

The painting shows an intimate interior. The three people in it are obviously very close friends. Jesus has had a long relationship with Mary and Martha, and he may have visited them often. Here, sitting at their table, he appears relaxed and comfortable in their home. Martha is busily preparing the food they are about to eat, while Mary sits at the feet of Jesus listening to him.

Notice how this depiction transcends time. All of the elements suggest a setting within Vermeer's culture and period. But Jesus remains clothed in the Middle Eastern garb of his time and place. The Jesus of history comes to them and meets them in their world. He does the same for us.

---

*On the Internet go to <www.essentialvermeer.com/catalogue/christ_in_the_house_of_mary_and_martha.jpg>.

The room is dark, serving to highlight the three dominant figures that are central to the story. The light brings them all into sharp focus. They are held closely in a large triangle, in the center of which is a brilliant white cloth, also a triangle. This artistic device invites us to enter and participate in the drama of the painting. Let us enter it together.

The text reminds us that when Jesus arrived at their house, Martha bustled about making preparations to receive this special guest. She was extending the hospitality that was normal and expected for the culture of Jesus' time by offering a meal. In the midst of her hurried preparations she noticed that Mary was sitting at Jesus' feet listening to him instead of helping her with the work. This is perfectly understandable to us. We too would feel irritated or even angry if we were left doing all the work when a guest visits, while others sit around without offering to help.

Then in her frustration and distraction, Martha approached Jesus and complained about the situation to him. She expressed her resentment to Jesus: "Lord, do You not care that my sister has left me to do all the serving alone? Then tell her to help me." It seemed so unfair to her that Mary got to sit and visit while Martha was left to the preparations alone. Jesus' response, at first seeming to carry a hint of impatience and scolding, was rather one of sadness and longing. He wanted Martha to join him and Mary in this warm circle of friendship.

Jesus acknowledged Martha's contribution to the "many things" that needed to be done. But he went on to tell her that she was too preoccupied with them and needed to do the "only one" necessary thing. That one thing was to be fully present to him and enjoy his company.

A CLOSER LOOK

Look at Martha in the painting. Her sleeves are pushed up to allow her to work unfettered by her clothing, which is plain and practical. In her hands she holds a basket of bread, which she probably baked herself. Martha's relationship with Jesus is obviously close and intimate enough for her to be totally honest with him about her feelings. Her culinary preparations suggest care and love for a very special friend. Yet Jesus is inviting something more from her. As she places her meal on the table, she turns her face to Jesus to express her concerns.

Jesus in turn looks at Martha but gestures toward Mary to indicate the one good thing that "shall not be taken away from her." It is an open, warm gesture which also communicates to Martha that she is included in it, if she will allow it. The interplay between the three figures creates a continuous movement between them in an otherwise still painting. The light and love on Jesus' face as he turns toward Martha expresses a tender and compassionate longing for fellowship with her too. Notice how his right hand, open and extended and highlighted by the bright white of the tablecloth, is not only pointing to Mary but is also a gentle invitation to spend time enjoying him. His hand seems to be offering the same invitation to us. How do you respond?

Whenever I heard this story I used to hear condemnation in Jesus' tone toward Martha. I am often a Martha in my busyness and willful effort to please God, and I long to be more like Mary and be more present to Jesus. Reflection on this painting has changed this for me. Now I hear a gentle invitation and longing in Jesus' words for me to come and sit at his feet and just be with him. I feel I can more readily and comfortably move in that direction because I know that my gifts to him are valued and I will not be rejected.

What does this one necessary thing look like? Let us turn our focus to Mary. She sits on a low stool at Jesus' feet. Her clothing is brighter and more colorful. Could it be something special she put on for this occasion? This could reflect her anticipation of his visit and her personal preparation for it. She sits in a relaxed manner, her left arm resting lightly on her left knee. Her right arm supports her face (reminiscent of Jesus' posture of contemplation in Moretto da Brescia's painting) as she leans slightly forward to attend to Jesus' words. Her feet are bare, suggestive of her humility and a visible symbol of a disciple.

Mary conveys to us an attitude of complete openness and receptivity to Jesus. She sits silently and attentively. Her position in the painting places her apart from Martha and the activities there. She seems almost isolated in her devotion. Her whole being is enraptured by Jesus. Like a child, there is nothing in her surroundings that distracts her from her single-minded, single-eyed absorption. Hers is a posture of natural, unforced devotion that flows out of a heart of love. She did not say, "I *must* have my quiet time alone with Jesus." For Mary, this was not a time that arose out of obligation or duty. Rather, she is caught up in her contemplation and looks to Jesus as a captivated lover would to her beloved. Her gaze is one that powerfully communicates to us the meaning of Christian contemplative prayer.

In Mary we see the elements of stillness, silence, solitude and an attentive heart. We have already acknowledged that it is not easy in our fast-paced world to enter into this contemplative space. Like Mary, we need to dispose ourselves to it, making the time and space to come apart from our busy, preoccupying activities. She shows us how to simply sit and be with God—free from distractions or idle chatter, analysis or self-examination to see what she is getting from the encounter. Free from these things, she has space for God and is left with just an adoring, attentive gaze.

Mary sits so close to Jesus that she seems to merge with him in the painting. Her knee seems to touch his. The shadowed rendering of their garments make little distinction between them. There is real physical and heart intimacy conveyed here. The vivid and sumptuously rendered tapestry behind Mary adds to the feeling of warmth and vitality in this relationship. This is a rich friendship that allows space for just being together.

Contemplative prayer allows her and us to listen with complete surrender to God. It is in this posture that we are enabled to really hear the voice of God. We need to be quiet, to stop talking and let ourselves be drawn into the silent mystery that is God. Notice that Mary and Jesus are right in the midst of the household activity. Jesus comes to us, communes with us, in the midst of our day-to-day existence. Our challenge is to be so attuned to him there that we can be drawn into a stillness of heart no matter what our surrounding circumstances. Practice in contemplative prayer cultivates this interior silence.

Jesus responds with inviting warmth to her attentions. At the same time he encourages Martha to leave aside her active absorption and consider choosing another way of relating to him. What Martha was preoccupied with was not unimportant or trivial. It was a necessary observance of cultural tradition and hospitality. It was her way of offering her gift of hospitality to Jesus. It was the way she expressed her love for him. Yet Jesus seems to be saying to her that as necessary as these things are, they must flow out of a posture and heart like Mary's—out of devotion and love.

All of our doing should flow out of being, and nothing grounds our being in God like being with God. Spending time in contemplative unworded stillness with God, even if it feels like wasting time, is prayer—because it is being with God. In a world that measures progress and rewards achievements, this way of being runs counter to the ways we have been conditioned to respond to God. Worded prayers of praise, worship and petitions to God are necessary to our faith life, but so often we neglect this equally important contemplative foundation of prayer. It is here, where we cease our talking and simply listen, that we can most easily discern the still, small voice of God. It is here that we can simply sit and gaze on our Beloved.

ℰ

FOR REFLECTION AND DISCUSSION

- Reread Luke 10:38-42 and then look again at Vermeer's painting. Place yourself within its frame. Who in the painting do you identify with at this moment? Where would you be? What would you be doing? What would you be thinking? As you look again at Martha, what would be in your basket—what are the preoccupations of your life, the "so many things" which worry and bother you, and which may lead you to avoid stillness before God? Now look at Jesus. What is he saying to you? How does he respond to the way you relate to him? What invitation is he extending to you now?

- What form would gazing on God take for you? How would you be led to respond if you were sitting in comfortable presence before God? What look would be on your face? What thoughts would be in your heart? How would it lead you back into the world, and how might you live your life there differently if you took this time more regularly to be with God in stillness?

- Ponder the psalmist's invitations to "be still, and know that I am God" (Psalm 46:10 NIV). Listen to this as an invitation rather than a command. Consider it as an invitation to be with God in stillness that allows you to know God through presence, not just words. Contemplative prayer begins by basking in the presence of our Beloved and then taking that presence with us as we live our daily lives in the world. If you hear an invitation to such being with God, speak with God about how you wish to respond. Consider also sharing this invitation and your planned response to it with someone you trust enough to share such things.

ATTUNED TO
GOD'S PRESENCE

Jean-François Millet
The Angelus

The kind of awareness that we have been considering to this point is prayer. It is an inner heart attitude of unbroken response to God's steadfast love and presence. Increased awareness of God can become a habitual way of life. It even holds the possibility of becoming ceaseless prayer, the sort of prayer encouraged by Paul in 1 Thessalonians 5:17-18, where he teaches that unending prayer is the will of God.

At first glance continuous prayer seems both impossible and impractical. Even faithful frequent prayer is difficult. How could we ever set aside an entire day for continuous prayer? We have families to care for, jobs to fulfill and livings to make. How much more impossible, it seems, would a life of ongoing ceaseless prayer be.

The problem, however, lies in our understanding of prayer. Rather than thinking of prayer as communicating with God, think of it as openness to God. Unceasing prayer is, then, unceasing openness to God. Think of what a difference it would make to our life if we were to live with a steady awareness of God's presence in the midst of our daily lived experience. This comes from a spirit that is turned toward God in openness and trusting attentiveness. It comes from a life that is grounded in unceasing prayer.

We are called to live in the world yet not be of it. To do this we need to be grounded in God and live with constant awareness of our relationship with God. This is what we see in the life of Jesus. He seemed to hardly be aware of himself as an individual. Always he spoke of himself *and* his Father. Nothing was more important to him than doing the will of his Father. Listen again to some of Jesus' familiar words:

- "I and the Father are one" (John 10:30).

- "For I did not speak on My own initiative, but the Father Himself who sent Me has given Me a commandment as to what to say and what to speak" (John 12:49).

- "He who has seen Me has seen the Father" (John 14:9).

- "Believe Me that I am in the Father and the Father is in Me" (John 14:11).

Jesus' relationship with the Father was the ground of his life. It was the core of his identity and the quiet center out of which he lived his life. And it is the center out of which we can live our lives.

Unceasing awareness of our relationship with God is, according to the testimony of the saints, possible. Millet's painting *The Angelus* presents us with a way to make it a reality in our lives. Read contemplatively, it offers us help in turning our attention and heart to the Lord as we pause to take in the wonder and mystery of Christ's life. But before we look at it, let us first consider the prayer it describes—the prayer known as "the Angelus."

Jean-François Millet (1814-1875)

Millet was born into a French peasant family, his parents working long hours each day as laborers in the fields. His love of nature and the Bible were instilled by a devout grandmother and parents who nurtured him in the faith.

Millet was particularly attracted to the beautiful engravings in the family Bible. These became the inspiration for many of his paintings as he used his artistic gifts to reproduce the world around him. His talent was recognized by his father and the parish priests, who provided him with the advantages of an excellent education. Steeped in mythology, Greek and Latin, Shakespeare and Milton, the literature of the classic spiritual mystics, and the Bible (which he called "the painter's book"), Millet was urged by his family to grow in his faith and to live so that "all your desire should be to praise God by thought, word and deed." His grandmother was a source of particular spiritual encouragement, telling Millet to "paint for eternity . . . and to never lose sight of the presence of God."

Many of Millet's paintings depicted the life of the peasant, causing him to be often called "the peasant painter." This was the world into which he was born, and he knew firsthand the hardships of working the land. The painting we are considering is very much a reflection of his personal childhood experience of observing this traditional prayer of his faith and culture. *The Angelus* (1857-1859) hangs in the Musée d'Orsay, Paris.

THE ANGELUS

Originating in the thirteenth century, the Angelus is a prayer practice that remains current for many Christians around the world. It is a practice that holds particular potential for all who seek to live a life of ceaseless prayer. The Angelus is a simple prayer, suitable for anyone who wants to learn to more regularly turn their attention toward God. Rich in doctrine and devotion, the Angelus commemorates the mystery of the incarnation. It is a biblical recollection of the angel Gabriel's visit to Mary to reveal to her that she had been chosen to bear the Christ child. The prayer itself included the angel's declaration to Mary—"And behold, you will conceive in your womb and bear a son, and you shall name Him Jesus" (Luke 1:31)—her response to this news— "Behold, the bondslave of the Lord; may it be done to me according to your word" (Luke 1:38), and a meditation on the Word made flesh from John 1:14—"the Word became flesh, and dwelt among us, and we saw His glory, glory as of the only begotten from the Father, full of grace and truth"—interspersed with the response of the "Hail Mary" prayer.

Traditionally, the Angelus was recited three times a day—at dawn, noon and dusk—each time being heralded by the ringing of the church bells. Their call prompted participants not only to stop their activities and respond with prayer but also to spread the good news of this salvific event to others. The ringing church bells were therefore a call to acknowledge and thank God for the saving work of Christ. Millet himself observed how his own father never failed to respond to the bells, stopping his work wherever he was, to pray the Angelus every day, "piously, hat in hand."

LOOKING AND LISTENING

Before proceeding, take a few moments to look carefully at Millet's *The Angelus.** Allow yourself sufficient time to enter the picture and notice as many of its features as you can. Be still before it, as if

---

*On the Internet go to <www.gardenofpraise.com/images/angelus4.jpg>.

you too have just now heard the church bells ring, calling you to prayer.

The painting presents two peasants in a field near the close of day. We also see the faint outline of a city behind them in the distance. Take note of the focus of the painting and the surrounding landscape. What is most striking to you about the people in the scene?

Millet's two peasants dominate the landscape, their monumental figures almost silhouetted against the flat farmland that surrounds them. This is a moment of deep and quiet reverence. All work has abruptly stopped as both the man and the woman stand in bowed silence while they reflect on the incarnation of Jesus, the meditation for the evening prayer. Privately each prays and meditates on the Scripture that reminds them of Mary's visit by the angel, where he tells her, "You will conceive in your womb and bear a son, and you shall name Him Jesus" (Luke 1:31). They ponder on the mystery of her willing surrender to God's will, and of the Word who was made flesh. The man, hat in hand, stands in devout humility and worship. The woman also bows her head, her hands tightly clasped in prayer close to her chest. It is an intensely private moment for each of them, yet their shared prayer unites them together in a holy alliance where God is present.

Notice the setting in which these two figures stand. At their feet is a large basket of potatoes, which they have temporarily left unattended to observe their evening ritual. Beside the man is his pitchfork, which he has set aside, stuck upright in the ground. Behind the woman stands a wheelbarrow with bags containing the fruit of their labors—freshly dug potatoes. In the misty distance we can see the spire of the village church emerging from the horizon. It would have been the bells from this steeple that summoned these people to prayer and announced the good news of the Word become flesh. The sky is golden with the light of the evening sun and barely visible birds flutter away in the right corner of the painting.

Everything in this work invites us to stillness and meditation.

The figures are immobile. The tools of their trade are abandoned. The landscape is completely flat and unpeopled except for these two who hold our attention. There is no movement at all, except for the barely visible birds in the distant sky. Time almost seems to stand still, and we become aware that this moment is special and sacred. This is not ordinary time—it transcends it. This moment of prayer transports these contemplatives into God's eternal *kairos* time. For these people of prayer, with the eyes of their heart turned toward God, the world has indeed grown dim, dissolved in heavenly light. The blaze of light behind them, symbolic of the radiant glory of God, seems to transfuse their humble daily tasks with dignity and nobility.

As we look at this painting, we can almost hear the fading echoes of the church bells that have prompted these people to pause for prayer. The warmth of the glowing evening sky that envelops this couple also reaches out to invite us to rest for a moment from our busy activities and turn our attention to God. Looking at this piece of art I find myself caught up in the quiet spaciousness of God's mercy and love. The devotional stillness and focus of the two figures draw me into silence. I feel attracted by the kind of faith shown here in these farmers. They invite me to take more frequent brief moments to look into the face of God as I go through my day.

TURNING OUR ATTENTION
TO GOD—RESPONDING

The practice of the Angelus prayer is a reminder of the value of setting aside specific times during the course of the day, as brief as these may be, to gently turn our attention toward God and acknowledge God's presence. If you live in an urban setting, it may be that church bells within your hearing already ring the Angelus. If not on the traditional hours, they may still ring regularly, and you can use the hearing of such ringing as a reminder to pause and turn your attention to God. Whatever you do in response to such a shift of your attention is prayer. You may silently speak God's name. Or you may simply offer an expression of thanks for God's presence. Any act of turning your attention to God is practice in the cultivation of ceaseless prayer.

But many things other than church bells can serve as such a reminder to turn your attention to God. Some people set a watch alarm to emit a small chirp each hour—using this as a reminder to turn toward God at these times. Starting with this simple action, Frank Laubach—a twentieth-century American missionary to the Philippines—then went on to set his alarm to sound at the beginning of every minute. After only four weeks of turning his attention to God for one second out of every waking minute of the day, he wrote, "I feel simply carried along each hour, doing my part in a plan which is far beyond myself. This sense of cooperation with God in little things is what so astonishes me, for I never have felt this way before." This is one man's attempt to pray without ceasing. For most of us it would be impractical. However, it does show the way we can cultivate attention to God. Doing so is one of the fruits of meditation on biblical art.

There are many other regular parts of a day that you can also use as a reminder to lift your heart and turn your attention toward God. You could, for example, do so each time you look into someone's face. Doing this could then become a prayer for them and an occasion of realignment of your own spirit with God's Spirit. Or you could do the same thing each time you pass through a door, turn a light off or on, or open a new email or text message. Consider the number of times in our day where we feel as if we are wasting time—times of waiting in airports, stalled in traffic jams, marking time as we wait to be called by the doctor or dentist, impatiently shuffling from one foot to the other until the next customer at the cashier's till is through, hovering near the entrance of our children's school for the bell to ring. These could become times where we turn our attention to God, where we offer up little expressions of gratitude or petitions, or simply notice where God is at that moment for us. By deliberately and consciously turning to God at regular times in our day we learn to make this the foundational rhythm of our life. We also begin to discover the extraordinary reality of divine presence in the midst of ordinary experience.

Practicing attentiveness throughout your day could also be cultivated by regularly expressing your gratitude to God for the gifts you receive. The more you do so, the more you will notice. You could begin by taking time at the end of the day to review your day and thank God for the blessings you received in it. Don't limit this to blessings that sound spiritual or religious. Simply take note of God in the midst of everyday experiences—the beauty of the natural world, the unexpected kindness of a stranger or friend, the expressive eyes of a street person, the playful laughter of a child, or the sound of music floating on the wind. Every experience offers us an opportunity to turn our heart toward the God who always yearns for fellowship with us. These are moments to express thanks for the gifts of God's loving presence and, by pausing in stillness and attentiveness, to allow God to transform your awareness. Frequent recollection of the gracious acts of God move us toward ceaseless prayer as our attention is more and more oriented toward God.

Thomas Green describes prayer as "an opening of the mind and heart to God." All that is necessary for prayer is for us to turn with trusting openness and attentiveness toward God. We may not have church bells that invite us to pause in the fields and pray, yet we can establish a rhythm of prayer within our day that allows us to cultivate unceasing prayer communion with God.

FOR REFLECTION AND DISCUSSION

- Return to Millet's *Angelus* and join the farmers in silence and stillness before God. Take some time to allow yourself to be drawn into the scene. Your life experience may be different from those depicted in the painting. But join the farmers in a moment of prayer. What do you experience as you stand in stillness with them with your heart open to God? What invitations to regular turning to God throughout your day do you experience as you do so?

- What calls to prayer could you build into your day as reminders to regularly turn toward God? How would you paint it if it were to show those reminders and the way you would like to respond? How would you look in that painting if it were to show your heart as you experience even those brief moments of communion with God?

- Consider also the practice of a daily review of your day, looking in the rearview mirror for signs of God's presence and gifts. A heart of gratitude toward God is a heart of prayer, and as your gratitude grows, so does a life of ceaseless prayer and continuous attentiveness to God develop.

- Finally, begin to practice this sort of attentiveness to God's presence throughout the flow of your day. Listen and look for God in the people around you, in the circumstances of your life and in the depth of your heart. Even if you have trouble discerning God's presence in circumstances and experiences, thank God for his loving presence and ask for help in more clearly discerning the God who truly is Immanuel—God with us.

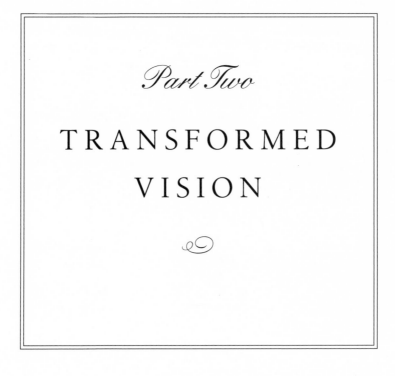

Part Two

TRANSFORMED VISION

CALLED TO SEE

NICOLAS POUSSIN

The Adoration of the Shepherds

*C*hristian spirituality is a journey into loving communion and union with God. It is learning to look into the face of God and, rather than experience guilt, fear or shame, know our belovedness.

We first catch a glimpse of the potential intimacy of God's relationship with humankind in the creation story found in Genesis. Adam and Eve were able to look upon the face of God and enjoy perfect fellowship with God. With pure eyes and in complete freedom they were able to walk and talk with God in the Garden of Eden. Nothing stood between them and God. But suddenly, on eating the fruit from the forbidden tree, their vision changed. Scriptures describe it as having their eyes opened, and they became aware that they were naked. But we could also say that their eyes were closed in that they lost awareness of their intimate communion with God. Their perfect relationship with God was broken and they suffered the consequences of their sin. From that moment on, God sought to restore the severed bond and heal their damaged seeing and knowing.

The Old Testament details the long and painful history of God's dealings with his people as he attempts to draw them closer. It is a story of a people who put their whole life in God's hands at one moment only to turn in the next toward unbelief. Their fickle journey was littered with the debris of their failure to trust God, on the one hand, and filled with God's corresponding acts of forgiveness and restoration, on the other. Many instances are recorded where the prophets, after personally seeing and responding to the glory of God in their own faith journey, called upon the Israelites to look upon, turn to and follow God. Moses told his people at the Red Sea to "stand by and see the salvation of the LORD" (Exodus 14:13). The Psalms resound with calls to behold the wonders of God's handiwork and to taste and see the goodness of God.

There is no end to the invitations to draw near and see God. If we make a habit of looking for God everywhere, we will begin to again discern these invitations. Awakened to the presence of God in our midst, and with eyes turned with expectancy toward God, we will be ready to hear and respond to the gifts of grace that fill our life. God continually invites us to come, to draw near and see for ourselves who God is. We can choose to accept, reject or ignore these invitations but they are always extended to us with the offer of love that transforms.

COME AND SEE—LISTENING

One of the most familiar invitations to come and see is that offered to the shepherds when the angelic host proclaimed the birth of their Messiah. Such news impelled them to hurry to Bethlehem to see for themselves what the angels were talking about. The entire account is found in Luke 2:8-20. Sit in a quiet place and prepare your heart and mind to receive it. Read the passage slowly and reflectively, noting the things that capture your attention. It may be a word or a phrase, an image, a sensation or a memory. Prayerfully attend to the invitation that it offers you to come and see.

In the same region there were *some* shepherds staying out in the fields and keeping watch over their flock by night.

And an angel of the Lord suddenly stood before them, and the glory of the Lord shone around them; and they were terribly frightened.

But the angel said to them, "Do not be afraid; for behold, I bring you good news of great joy which will be for all the people;

for today in the city of David there has been born for you a Savior, who is Christ the Lord.

This *will be* a sign for you: you will find a baby wrapped in cloths and lying in a manger."

And suddenly there appeared with the angel a multitude of the heavenly host praising God and saying,

"Glory to God in the highest,

And on earth peace among men with whom He is pleased."

When the angels had gone away from them into heaven, the shepherds *began* saying to one another, "Let us go straight to Bethlehem then, and see this thing that has happened which the Lord has made known to us."

So they came in a hurry and found their way to Mary and Joseph, and the baby as He lay in the manger.

When they had seen this, they made known the statement which had been told them about this Child.

And all who heard it wondered at the things which were told them by the shepherds.

But Mary treasured all these things, pondering them in her heart.

The shepherds went back, glorifying and praising God for all that they had heard and seen, just as had been told them.

Now turn to the painting by the French classicist artist Nicolas Poussin, titled *The Adoration of the Shepherds,* and take a long,

---

Nicolas Poussin (1594-1665)

Nicolas Poussin, one of the founders of European classicism, was considered to be the most influential and greatest French artist of the seventeenth century. After some studies in France, he traveled to Italy, where he was greatly influenced by the Venetian artists. He spent much of his life in Rome, except for two years serving as court painter to Louis XIII. He acquired a great admiration for ancient Roman civilization, spending much of his time drawing from the ancient statues that were everywhere in his adopted country.

Educated by monks, Poussin was well-grounded in the teachings of his faith as a young boy. The Bible stories would have been very familiar to him, and in his middle years he produced many paintings based on biblical events. *The Adoration of the Shepherds* was painted between 1633 and 1634 and is found in the National Gallery of London. Painting for the Counter-Reformation, Poussin's works illustrated the spiritual meanings of his subjects. His religious themes were chosen for their pageantry and drama, and although classical in clarity and monumentality, they were never cold or lifeless. Rather, his paintings told a story whose figures radiated a life and vitality all their own through their gestures and facial expressions.

slow look.* Painted sometime around 1634, it depicts the event found in Luke 2:15-16: "When the angels had gone away from them into heaven, the shepherds *began* saying to one another, 'Let us go straight to Bethlehem then, and see this thing that has happened which the Lord has made known to us.' So they came in a hurry and found their way to Mary and Joseph, and the baby as He lay in the manger." As you meditated on this text, what images emerged for you? Where were you in the scene? What did you see and hear?

LOOKING

Perhaps your picture of these events takes place in the dark interior of a barn. Maybe you recall paintings by other artists that place the holy family in a rough structure surrounded by straw and farm animals—a humble beginning for a king. But in Poussin's painting we see this event taking place in the open air. Here, shepherds bow in adoration before the Christ child as angelic beings hover delicately above them. There is no stable, just a crumbling structure that was once grandly supported by classical Doric columns.

The painting is perfectly composed, well-balanced and ordered, with clearly defined lines which mirror the clarity of pure faith. All of the figures are carefully placed in frieze-like fashion on the canvas. The composition of the two main groups takes our eyes across the painting from left to right and then moves us in and back toward the landscape beyond. The blue cloak of the woman on the far left visually connects her with Mary and also keeps our eyes focused where they should be—on the Christ child. Look at the hidden triangles that underlie the cherubs, the adoring shepherds and the holy family. They serve the same purpose of giving unity and visual focus to the work. Yet the scene is not static or formally stiff. Structural order and symmetry are offset by vitality and po-

---

*On the Internet go to <www.abcgallery.com/P/poussin/poussin24.JPG>.

etic tenderness in the people who occupy its space. The flowing
fabric of the shepherd in blue seems to be lifted by the wind to indicate her haste in making this pilgrimage. All the faces and gestures demonstrate eagerness, love and awe at what they see.

Take some time to look more closely at the painting. To what
are your eyes first drawn as you look? What is the focal point?
What is the direction of each person's gaze?

Notice that all the attention is focused on Jesus. He is the focal
point. All eyes look toward the Word, who has been made flesh—
the Word we now can see. The chubby feet of the angels point
downward in a line which, if continued, draws our eyes along the
right pillar toward Christ—an artistic device to point us to the
most important part or person in the painting.

On one obvious level the painting is about the shepherds coming to worship the baby Jesus, but on another level it is about seeing. Even the donkey has its eyes trained on Jesus, who is bathed
in glowing light. Here is the light of the world, his tiny body ac-
centuated by the white swaddling cloth held by his mother. He lies
in a crude basket that is filled with straw. Both Mary and Joseph
lean toward the child, who is also the focus of their wonder and
adoration. It all happens in a very ordinary and lowly place. There
is nothing spectacular to see here to match the shining array of
angels who first conveyed the news. Yet had the shepherds ignored
the heavenly visitors, had they refused to see, they would have
missed this glorious revelation of God made flesh.

Behind the donkey two men have also traveled to be witnesses
to this birth. They gesture with hands and head as they talk with
each other about what they are seeing. Looking through the pillars
and further back into the painting we see another group of shepherds who are looking upward to the skies, which still glow from
the light of the retreating angelic host. They seem overwhelmed
and frightened by their experience as they shield themselves in different ways from the brilliance of the heavenly glory. Recall their

response to the appearance of the angels as they tended their sheep—"they were terribly frightened." Encounters with God could be terrifying because they bring us face to face with the transcendent majesty and holiness of God. Yet, in Jesus, God comes to us and sends his angels to announce that he is approachable. We no longer need to be afraid to draw near to God. Now we are invited simply to come, see and worship. The upright figure with his blue cloak over his head appears to be either fleeing or starting on his journey toward the manger. How would you respond to such an awesome angelic encounter—with flight or with receptivity?

The artist presents the enormous importance of these events in several ways. He sets his scene in a framework of classical architecture. But notice that it is in decay, cracking and crumbling in places. Stones have fallen from its masonry and lie strewn on the ground before the shepherds. The old-world system is crumbling and passing away to be replaced by a new and better one. The woman in bright blue on the left side of the painting carries a large basket of fruit as an offering to Jesus. She is also part of the old classical world and prompts us to think of pagans or shepherdesses bringing their offerings of fruit and flowers to their gods. Christ's coming has inaugurated a new age, a new covenant, that supersedes the old. But how is his new kingdom going to be realized? Return your gaze to the wooden crossbeam that separates the angels from the humans below. If you look closely you may see that it suggests the shape of a cross. Could the artist be making a subtle reference to the future work of Christ? The new covenant would only be made possible and effective through the life, death and resurrection of Christ.

SEEING THAT TRANSFORMS—RESPONDING

What then is the point of all this seeing? Isaiah 7:14 tells us: "Behold [look], a virgin will be with child and bear a son, and she will call His name Immanuel." God has stooped, humbled himself and taken on human flesh. With Jesus' incarnation God is with us. God has come near to us and now invites us to draw near to him. Jesus' coming is not just for a select few but for all humanity, and to redeem all of creation. The infant Jesus, utterly naked and vulnerable, lies in the humblest manger—a sign to us of God's availability to us. God can now be not only seen but touched. The shepherds in this scene are close enough to touch the child, and we can perhaps imagine them stooping further to the point of actually reaching out and touching him in awe and reverence. The one closest to Jesus is almost there. Their gestures clearly convey their emotional response.

I feel compelled to join these shepherds in their worshipful response to Jesus. Looking at them, I am drawn to the one at the front of the line, closest to Jesus. He seems to be in the most fortunate position of being close enough to touch the child. He pulls me into the painting to reach out and touch this small, shining wonder that is the baby Jesus. But he also causes me to think about what my best gifts would be that I could bring as an offering of gratitude and love. A verse from Christina Rossetti's Christmas poem "In the Bleak Midwinter" (1872) beautifully expresses the longing that I sense from entering into this painting:

> What can I give him,
> poor as I am,
> If I were a shepherd,
> I would bring a lamb.
> If I were a wise man,
> I would do my part.
> Yet what I can, I give him—
> Give my heart.

Compare and contrast this group of adoring shepherds to the blind men in the first painting at the beginning of the book. Both groups share a similar structural triangular shape of stooping bodies that gradually fall forward. But there is a vast difference between the figures—one group bends forward with intentionality to receive life and to worship. The other group seems to hurtle forward in chaos toward a headlong death. In Poussin's painting, the eyes of the shepherds are open, focused and full of light as the light of Jesus radiates toward them. The men in Bruegel's painting have eyes that are blind to spiritual truth and their lives are full of gloom. Jesus said that if your eye is full of light or healthy, your whole body will be full of light. Clearly we see how this is true as we look at both these paintings. Transformed seeing brings light, life and growth.

In his book *Prayers for a Lifetime,* Karl Rahner reminds us of the meaning of Immanuel. He says, "To live within the near past-all-graspness of God . . . is at once terrifying and blissful. But we have no choice. God is with us." See the differing reactions of fear and positive responsiveness by the shepherds to the angelic visitors in the painting. Yes, we are filled with fear, awe and trembling when we meet God. But in Jesus—Immanuel—God comes near enough to us to be touched and felt without fear. Jesus is God for us at all times—in our past, present and future. God's desire is for us to be free enough to allow ourselves to be found by the One who wants to be with us and to have us live with and in him forever.

Our seeing, our gazing in attentiveness and openness, has a purpose. Its ultimate end is to lead us to respond to God and in that response to be changed into people of faith. In the story presented in this painting, the act of seeing draws the shepherds into worship and adoration. They have responded to the invitation to draw near. Now they can return to their everyday life as witnesses to God's grace. Their lives have been transformed by their seeing. They go back into their daily experience filled with the wonder and blessing of sharing in and being part of God's astounding entrance in their lives. The text tells us that they went home rejoicing at the wondrous things they had heard and seen. In turn those who heard their message also marveled at the Christ.

Transformation happens when we attend to God's gentle wooing. Turning toward God with renewed vision and a heart that dares to be open, we find that we are made anew. God gives us a heart of flesh instead of a heart of stone. We become people who dare to allow God to mold us more and more into the image of Christ. Responding to God with trust and allowing God's life to flow through us becomes a transforming habit.

FOR REFLECTION AND DISCUSSION

- How do you respond to God's invitation to come and see the salvation of the Lord (Exodus 14:13)? You do not have to wait until Christmas to join the shepherds and once again witness the wondrous event through which the Lord has been made known to us. To help you do so, return to the Poussin painting. Notice the large rock just in front of the cradle. What does it suggest to you? Perhaps it points to God, the rock of our salvation. Or possibly it represents a stumbling block that keeps you from drawing closer. What are those things that keep you from drawing near and seeing? God's desire is that we come close enough to gaze upon God's face. In so doing we know who we are and where we belong. With the shepherds, bow down and worship the God who has taken on our flesh.

- In the incarnation God redeemed not only humankind but all of creation. He lifted up humanity into the divine life, giving us back our dignity. In the ordinary, smelly stable, the sacred and profane were brought together, making the humblest things holy and exalted. Are you able to see the sacred in the meanest things in life? Do you recognize the Christ child in the ordinary circumstances of your life? If not, what keeps you from seeing?

- What gifts and invitations do you receive as you pause to see the Christ? How has your vision begun to be transformed by meditating on this text and painting? Where do you place your focus, and what is your response?

6

IMMANUEL,
GOD WITH US

REMBRANDT
Christ in the Storm on the Lake of Galilee

*G*od's nearness and approachability are clearly revealed in the person of Jesus. As he lived and walked on this earth, responding to people and inviting them to follow him, he embodied Immanuel. Jesus voluntarily gave up all the privileges of his divine office so that he could fully identify with human beings. This identification was so complete that he experienced all the vicissitudes common to humanity—joy, tears, distress, temptations, pain, sorrow and rejection.

The band of men who were Jesus' closest followers saw firsthand this God made flesh and his dealings with people. They may not have recognized that he was the Christ, who would redeem Israel, but they witnessed his interactions with others as he ministered his grace to them—healing the sick, opening blind eyes, casting out demons, raising the dead and associating with the outcasts of society. They must have puzzled over his inclusive embrace of all human beings. But they were constantly attracted to him and saw for themselves the way he responded to their own lot in life.

There are times when we have no trouble at all seeing God and his action in our lives—times of blessing, order, peace or joy. It is when life becomes chaotic, disordered or burdensomely troubled, when we are at our wit's end that we cry out to God asking where he is. We may sometimes feel abandoned by God when we are in this state. It is at such times that it is most difficult to discern God's presence and power in our lives. Yet Scripture assures us that God will never leave us nor forsake us, that God loves us with such a fierce love that nothing can separate us from that love.

The psalmist prays to God in Psalm 119:66—"Teach me good discernment and knowledge, for I believe in Your commandments." Central to Ignatian spirituality is the practice of the examen—a prayer of discernment at the end of each day, which helps us to see the ways God has been present or absent from our daily lives. This prayer of attending to God's presence, when practiced regularly, opens our eyes to new ways of recognizing God's interruptions, God's attempts to catch our attention, through our day. It is a prayer that sharpens our awareness and clears our vision so that we learn to discern where God is in our lives every day.

Briefly, the examen takes the form of sitting in silence and stillness when the day is over, asking God to show us where he has been in our life and thanking God for those times. In that same contemplative posture, ask God where you have missed or ignored his presence. Then ask for forgiveness for those times and for help to do better the next day in being more aware.

AT SEA WITH THE LORD—LISTENING

What if the disciples who were tossed about on the stormy Sea of Galilee were to have practiced this examen at the end of their frightening day? Would they have looked back and recognized that Jesus, the one who is Lord of the winds and the waves, was with

Rembrandt van Rijn (1633-1669)

Rembrandt was born in Leiden, the Netherlands. A very successful artist with many commissioned works, Rembrandt is considered to be the greatest artist of the Dutch school. His masterful use of light and dark, especially in his religious masterpieces, capture not only the drama of biblical events but the psychological and spiritual mood as well. One third of the total body of his works are depictions of religious or biblical subjects.

Living his life in a seafaring nation, Rembrandt knew well the power of the sea and the dramatic storms of the northern European coasts. His interpretation of Jesus asleep in the boat in the storm reflects his personal experience of this. Burdened with familial and financial pressures, with personal misfortunes and sorrows later in life, Rembrandt vividly depicts the inner emotional drama of the disciples in his painting. We cannot see clearly in this print all of the details, but it seems that Rembrandt has inscribed his own name on the rudder of the boat. Could he be reflecting his own place in this boat and his own response to Jesus' question addressed to the disciples?

Christ in the Storm on the Lake of Galilee, 1633, is supposedly Rembrandt's only seascape. It is fairly large—5.3 feet by 4.2 feet—and belongs to the Isabella Stewart Garner Museum in Boston. Unfortunately, this painting was stolen in 1990 and has not yet been recovered.

them from the start, and would they have regretted their lack of faith? How would they have responded if they had recognized that Jesus, who was with them, was able to still the turbulent waters? Would they have turned to him for help earlier?

Rembrandt's depiction of the story expresses the disciples' terror and panic during the storm on the Sea of Galilee. "And there arose a fierce gale of wind, and the waves were breaking over the boat so much that the boat was already filling up. Jesus Himself was in the stern, asleep on the cushion" (Mark 4:37-38).

Turn to the story in the Gospel of Mark 4:35-41. Read it slowly and contemplatively, placing yourself in the boat with the terrified disciples, entering fully into the story. Notice what insights come to your attention, staying with whatever gifts God gives you, and be thankful.

On that day, when evening came, He said to them, "Let us go over to the other side."

Leaving the crowd, they took Him along with them in the boat, just as He was; and other boats were with Him.

And there arose a fierce gale of wind, and the waves were breaking over the boat so much that the boat was already filling up.

Jesus Himself was in the stern, asleep on the cushion; and they woke Him and said to Him, "Teacher, do You not care that we are perishing?"

And He got up and rebuked the wind and said to the sea, "Hush, be still." And the wind died down and it became perfectly calm.

And He said to them, "Why are you afraid? Do you still have no faith?"

They became very much afraid and said to one another, "Who then is this, that even the wind and the sea obey Him?"

Mark's account situates this event after Jesus had been teaching the multitude and his disciples about the kingdom of God. They had left the crowd to go to the other side of the Sea of Galilee in a boat. On their way there "a fierce gale of wind" arose and "the waves were breaking over the boat so much that the boat was already filling up." Through all this turmoil Jesus, probably exhausted from his day full of teaching and interacting with the multitudes, fell asleep on a pillow. His terrified disciples shook him awake, and with voices full of puzzlement, possibly rebuke, they asked: "Teacher, do You not care that we are perishing?" These words remind us of Martha's complaint as she expressed her frustration at Mary's sitting with Jesus instead of helping in the kitchen.

Once awakened, Jesus immediately stilled the wind and the high seas with his words, "Hush, be still." As calm returned and peace was restored, he penetrated their questioning hearts. He asked them: "Why are you afraid? Do you still have no faith?" At this, their fear returned but it was a different fear. It was an awesome fear of the One whom the wind and the sea obey.

TAKING TIME TO CONTEMPLATE—LOOKING

Now turn your attention to Rembrandt's painting of this scene, *Christ in the Storm on the Lake of Galilee.** Take some time to look carefully at the details of the event as depicted here. With your own imagination animated by your reading of the text, notice what most immediately and powerfully grabs your attention. How does the scene formed in your mind shift or change as you look at this painting?

Initially, you may have been struck by the dramatic use of light and dark that divides the canvas into two distinct parts. To emphasize this contrast, the towering mast, resembling a cross,

---

*On the Internet go to <www.abcgallery.com/R/rembrandt/rembrandt99.html>.

pitches upward in a powerful diagonal. On the left is the brighter, stormier side. On the right it is very dark, yet there seems to be some stillness where Jesus is. These contradictions of light and dark cause us to pause and consider their implications for us.

Let us first look at the left half of the painting. The boat heaves on the crest of a massive wave, churning from the gale-force winds. Rembrandt theatrically captures on his canvas the wind-whipped waves, foaming white, and the spewing spray in the yellow light. He anchors the story in his own time and place with a boat that looks very much like the fishing vessels of his era. It is tossed about so much that some of its rigging seems to have snapped off and is flapping around high overhead.

The men on the foredeck wrestle and struggle to keep the boat from capsizing. The disciples themselves are blown about by the winds, the one working on the central mast trying for all his worth to reattach the violently torn and tattered mainsail that seems to be about to be whipped off. An oar and grappling hook flail about as well, about to be lost to the waves. We can almost hear the savage flapping of sails and cloaks, the creaking of masts and hull, and the howling whistle of the tempestuous winds. In this depiction by Rembrandt, it is easy for us to enter into the palpable horror and terror experienced by the disciples.

Severe storms such as this one were common on the Sea of Galilee. They were known to spring up out of nowhere under the calmest conditions and burst into action, dashing any unfortunate sailing vessels into its depths. Rembrandt stays true to the text, showing the waves rising up over the front of the boat and beginning to fill it. The light on the left side of the painting, illuminating the thunderous clouds above, is an eerie yellow. It highlights the plight of the men on board as they grapple with the uncontrollable elements. We would expect to find Jesus in this brighter side of the painting. But look at where he sleeps.

Rembrandt places Jesus in the shadowed side of the painting.

Though he is in the dark, he is still available and can be touched—he is Immanuel, God with us in the flesh. He is being shaken awake on the shoulder by one of the disciples. Others look intently at Jesus as they await his reaction to their situation. Another sits with tiller in hand and tries to steady the boat. One in the foreground leans over the side of the boat. Perhaps he is checking out the damaged condition of the boat, or possibly he is seasick, vomiting over the edge.

In spite of the darkness the faces of the men on this side are lit by the same eerie yellow light. On this side of the gigantic wave, it is relatively calm. Compared to the turbulence in the front of the boat, it is quiet here. The panic that is externally expressed in the men in the bright half seems to be more internalized here in the darker half of the painting. We do not catch a sense of the terror in their postures. It seems to be more of a focused intentionality in their action of waking Jesus. Notice in the text that they do not ask Jesus to calm the storm, but appear angry at his seemingly uncaring attitude to them. Could their postures convey a sense of reproach toward Jesus?

Jesus is perfectly at peace in the stern of the boat and sleeps soundly during this terrific storm. His total trust in his heavenly Father stands in stark contrast to the frantic struggles of his disciples. His question to them about their lack of faith is an invitation to them to abandon control, to trust him completely and not be afraid. His question to them is also a question to us in whatever distress we might be experiencing. "Why do you fear? Why do you have no faith? How long will you wait before turning to me for help?" Far from being uncaring or aloof, Jesus is actually in the boat with his disciples. He is in our boat too. If you count the number of men in the boat and look really hard, you may see what looks like the figure of a thirteenth disciple (at the feet of Jesus and to the immediate left of the figure in red who seems to be seasick). Who could this person be, and why would the artist have included him? Is it possible that the artist had inserted himself into the painting to personalize it? He was known to do this in some of his works, a common practice for many artists of that time. Or may it also be a way to include us in the scene by inviting us to take on the personality of the unrecognized participant? Whatever his reasons, it gives us pause to consider our response to this story.

I have always had both a fascination and a fear of the ocean. This painting brings back a traumatic childhood memory, and I respond to it with terror. Growing up on a small Caribbean island, I knew the violent and uncontrollable power of the sea. I remember once standing on the beach watching helplessly as several members of my family were swept out to sea by a rip tide (they were rescued safely). Later in life I have had scary moments not only when swimming in the ocean but also sailing in boats on rough waters. So it is easy for me to identify with the frightened disciples in the groaning ship on their turbulent sea. Like them, I still have a difficult time hearing a gentle invitation from Jesus, rather than a rebuke, to trust him in the middle of this storm when I know he could make things calm again with just one word. I too question his slow response for help. The stormy sea still holds terror for me, but as I see him lying in the shadows of my own boat, the invitation to me is to let go and surrender to his love and safety. He invites me to trust that he is there in the turmoil even when I sense him the least. He waits there for me to turn my eyes and heart toward him.

RESPONDING

Pause for a moment and reflect on where Jesus is in the boat that is your present life. You may have trouble seeing in the dark or you may find that your situation is exposed to the glaring light of day. Is Jesus asleep or unconcerned? Is he present in the darkness? What does the light reveal to you about your own struggles to stay afloat?

With the cruciform mast looming high overhead and casting its shadow over the dark side of the painting, we are reminded of Psalm 107:23-30, where the psalmist describes the perils of the sea and the terror of the sailors who stagger like drunken men and are "at their wits' end" as the boat heaves about in the stormy waves. At the same time we may also recall that the Scriptures remind us that to God, darkness and light are the same. He is present in both if we would only recognize him and turn to him in faith and trust. Our safety and deliverance are only found beneath the shadow of his cross. We need eyes to see God even in our darkest and stormiest experiences of life.

FOR REFLECTION AND DISCUSSION

- Return your attention to the painting. Put yourself in the boat with the disciples. Where would you be in the boat? What sounds do you hear? What does it feel like to be in such a storm?

- In each of our lives, storms are inevitable. What are the storms in your life at this moment? Does God seem uninvolved, absent or asleep during your struggles? Are you ever tempted to lose faith during these times?

- What are you afraid of today? How can you discern the presence of God in the midst of this? Imagine yourself as one of the men in the boat who shakes Jesus awake. What are his words to you personally? How do you respond to him?

- Pause for a few moments to review your day. Where do you notice God's presence or absence in it? Thank him for the times where you recognized him. Ask forgiveness for the times you may have missed or ignored God. Ask for the gift of discernment to see God in your day tomorrow. Live each day with the assurance that Jesus is constantly with you in every aspect of your life—in joy and in pain—and allow him to take the helm of control over your life.

- Allow yourself to prayerfully reflect on the words of a hymn by Charles Wesley.

Lord of earth, and air, and sea,
Supreme in power and grace,
Under thy protection, we
Our souls and bodies place.
Bold an unknown land to try,
We launch into the foaming deep;
Rocks, and storms, and deaths defy,
With Jesus in the ship.

Who the calm can understand
In a believer's breast?
In the hollow of his hand
Our souls securely rest:
Winds may rise, and seas may roar,
We on his love our spirits stay;
Him with quiet joy adore,
Whom winds and seas obey.

As you become aware of the state of your own soul in the midst of struggle, allow these words to penetrate deep into your heart. Rest in the assurance that the peace and calm that Jesus promises to those who seek him will be yours as well. Worship him who controls the wind and the waves, and rest in his love.

7

SEEING AND BELIEVING

CARAVAGGIO
The Incredulity of St. Thomas

*T*he followers of Jesus experienced unimaginable dismay and fear after his death on the cross. He seemed to have disappeared from the tomb and to have vanished completely from their sight. Yet how like Jesus not to leave them in despair and hopelessness! He made several appearances to his disciples after his resurrection to reassure them of his continuing presence and love. In one such appearance he came to them in a room where they were hiding behind locked doors. It is no wonder that they were afraid and hid themselves. If this kind of death happened to Jesus, it was a possibility for them too for having associated themselves with him. It was in this hiding place that Jesus appeared to them like a ghost.

What a shock this must have been when Jesus suddenly appeared like a specter in their upper-room hideout. His looks were not at all like the Messiah that they were expecting. He did not come to them as a conquering, triumphant hero. He came still bearing the wounds of his crucifixion. But this was not an otherworldly phantom but a tangible, solid body. It was only when he spoke to them his peace and showed them his hands and his side that they recognized who he was, leading them to rejoice in his living, continuing presence.

ENTERING THE UPPER ROOM—LISTENING

The account tells us that Thomas was not present with the others at that moment, and later, when he heard from them that they had seen Jesus, he refused to believe. He maintained that "unless I see in His hands the imprint of the nails, and put my finger into the place of the nails, and put my hand into His side, I will not believe" (John 20:25). Jesus, ever persistent in drawing people to himself, returned to the same locked room eight days later when Thomas was present, taking the initiative to respond to his doubt. He stood among the disciples and addressed Thomas directly, "Reach here with your finger, and see My hands; and reach here your hand and put it into My side; and do not be unbelieving, but believing" (John 20:27).

Settle into a comfortable, quiet place and spend some time prayerfully reading this entire story as found in John 20:19-29. Pay close attention to the details of the place where it all happens. Be present with the disciples as they hide in the room. Place yourself in the story and notice what the experience is like to be in hiding, fearful for your life. Listen to the conversations that occur, and notice your own responses. What do you feel when Jesus suddenly appears and walks like a ghost through the locked door? And what is your response when Jesus speaks to you and shows you his wounds?

> So when it was evening on that day, the first day of the week, and when the doors were shut where the disciples were, for fear of the Jews, Jesus came and stood in their midst and said to them, "Peace be with you."
>
> And when He had said this, He showed them both His hands and

His side. The disciples then rejoiced when they saw the Lord.

So Jesus said to them again, "Peace be with you; as the Father has sent Me, I also send you."

And when He had said this, He breathed on them and said to them, "Receive the Holy Spirit.

"If you forgive the sins of any, their sins have been forgiven them; if you retain the sins of any, they have been retained."

But Thomas, one of the twelve, called Didymus, was not with them when Jesus came.

So the other disciples were saying to him, "We have seen the Lord!" But he said to them, "Unless I see in His hands the imprint of the nails, and put my finger into the place of the nails, and put my hand into His side, I will not believe."

After eight days His disciples were again inside, and Thomas with them. Jesus came, the doors having been shut, and stood in their midst and said, "Peace be with you."

Then He said to Thomas, "Reach here with your finger, and see My hands; and reach here your hand and put it into My side; and do not be unbelieving, but believing."

Thomas answered and said to Him, "My Lord and my God!"

Jesus said to him, "Because you have seen Me, have you believed? Blessed are they who did not see, and yet believed."

BEING THERE—LOOKING

Now turn your attention to Caravaggio's meditation on this significant moment. The painting is called *The Incredulity of St. Thomas.** Take a few moments to look at this stunning piece of art.

---

*On the Internet go to <www.abcgallery.com/C/caravaggio/caravaggio34.html>.

Caravaggio (1571-1610)

Known today by his birthplace, Caravaggio was born Michelangelo Merisi on September 28, 1573, in Caravaggio, Italy. Considered to be one of Italy's greatest seventeenth-century painters, the young artist was inspired by the works of Raphael and Michelangelo. After working for private patrons for several years, he moved to Rome, where he was commissioned to produce paintings for the Contarelli Chapel of the church of San Luigi dei Francesi. *The Incredulity of St. Thomas* (1601-1602) is now housed in the Sanssouce, in Potsdam, Germany.

Caravaggio's art was revolutionary. Scorning the traditional idealized interpretation of religious subjects, he presented the real world—common things and common people painted with passion and empathy. Using models from real life, he placed them in settings made dramatic and evocative by his use of the technique called *chiaroscuro*—the dramatic use of light and dark. Using selective illumination of form out of deep shadow, he brought the viewer face to face with the supernatural in the midst of the natural.

Painting from life directly onto his canvas without an initial drawing, Caravaggio's passionate, spontaneous style reflected his own life. A controversial and hot-tempered figure, Caravaggio lived recklessly. Frequently seen in public with a drawn sword, he was involved in fights, was imprisoned on several occasions and eventually had to flee as a fugitive from Rome. He died lonely and abandoned at the age of thirty-nine. Yet his works stand as powerful, lasting reminders of the gifts and graces of God.

What is your first reaction to it? What is the first thing to which your eyes are drawn? The canvas displays a remarkable treatment of light and dark. Four characters occupy the space in a very dark room, their bodies forming an architectural arch that holds them together in a compact knot. The figures are ordinary yet monumental, and fill the space of the canvas. They crowd into a tightly packed huddle around Jesus, their attention riveted by what they see—Thomas's finger being pushed into the wound in Jesus' side.

Let's look at the focal point of the painting. Caravaggio's masterful use of light and dark brings this story into spellbinding attention. A miraculous light floods in from somewhere on the left of the scene. This light, coming from an unknown source, is a signal to us by the artist that this is a supernatural event. It illuminates the person who holds this moment of tension together and around whom all the participants cluster—the resurrected Jesus. Jesus' body is glaringly exposed, revealing his vulnerability and his humanity. His flesh still bears the yellowish pallor of the grave and stands in marked contrast to the strong, sunburned vigor of the former fishermen. This is a very real, very human body—not a ghost or an apparition. The resurrection is a reality. Jesus' promise to be present with us at all times suddenly becomes a lived truth for these disciples.

Some sadness seems to be present in Jesus' facial expression. Could it be a response to Thomas's doubt? Or could it be a response to the physical pain this action of Thomas may have caused Jesus? In his attempt to depict the reality of the resurrection with all of its implied physicality, Caravaggio presents Jesus' body as it emerges out of the shadows, this emphasizing that he is human but yet not completely knowable. There is more here than we can grasp. There is awe and mystery here we must respond to.

Notice that it is Jesus who initiates this encounter. He does not chastise or condemn Thomas for doubting, but with his left hand he gently takes Thomas's hand and guides it toward the wound in his side. His right hand pulls back his clothing to expose his body even more, in all its vulnerability, to the light of revelation, which will dispel the darkness of doubt. His gesture suggests both gentleness and firmness. Notice that the nail wound is visible in Jesus' guiding hand. He goes even further and seems to thrust it forward into the gash itself. Look at how deeply his finger reaches into the wound. Our reaction to this powerfully realistic depiction when we first looked at it may have been "Ouch!" Caravaggio portrays the wound as still raw and fresh. Surely this would cause Jesus pain when Thomas's finger pokes it.

Look at where the eyes of all the characters in this scene are focused. While Jesus and the two other disciples look at Thomas's hand, Thomas seems to have his attention focused elsewhere, slightly beyond the main event. His eyes are somewhat averted from the wound, even from his own hand. He avoids looking directly at the wound, which he loudly pronounced he would touch before he could believe. There is incredulity and some degree of awe in his look—possibly fear at the prospect of touching the holy. He holds his left arm at his side, seeming to tentatively pull back from Jesus, another indication of his hesitancy. We are drawn further into the story by his highlighted shoulder and the patch of white on his elbow—an elbow that projects out into our viewing space. It forces us to look at our own doubts and responses to Jesus' living presence in the midst of our ordinary lives. As we questioned whether or not we would run to see the baby Jesus in the manger, here we are compelled to consider how readily we would reach out and touch Jesus if he appeared physically in our midst.

BRINGING OUR DOUBTS TO JESUS—RESPONDING

Thomas was also called Didymus, which means the twin. There seem to be two people in Thomas—the doubter and the believer. One part of him doubted that Jesus was actually alive from the dead and the other believed enough to seek out the community he was a part of. He knew where to find the others. They would have been bound together through their previously shared common stories and memories, their collective history and language. Remember the number of times when Jesus lived among them when Thomas questioned Jesus about his words—his promise to prepare a mansion for those who believe, his returning to the Father, and Thomas's expression of going with Jesus to die with him. His is a questioning, pondering faith that does not take things at face value. He does not flatly deny that Jesus was present in the room, but he demands hard evidence. He had seen his Lord brutally tortured and crucified, and he can't understand how it could be true that he yet lives. The horrors of the death of his friend are still immediate and real. If Jesus was indeed alive, then Thomas knew that he was the kind of person who would still bear the wounds that would provide the proof that he needed.

Thomas's own vulnerability was soothed and comforted by touching Jesus. He received assurance that Jesus holds him and cares for him. This assurance can also be true for us. Even though we may hide or deny them, our wounds are signs of our humanity. But healing for us comes from the very wounds of Jesus if we too dare to touch him and allow ourselves to be touched by him. Jesus is still tied to the wounded humanity he came to redeem. Because of this we can be assured that we and all of creation are held in his wounded hands.

Thomas returned to his community because this was where he knew he would find strength and encouragement in his faith. This is the community Jesus himself had created around him and which he had nurtured by his presence when he walked on the earth. It is also where Christ now appears and brings renewed faith to us. We are all like Thomas with these two opposing sides to our character. It is within the community of faith where we find support and encouragement to keep the doubter in each one of us from crushing our belief.

The faces of the two other disciples are shown with the same degree of wonder and doubt. Crowded together on the canvas, all their heads are united in their quest for truth. Eyebrows shoot up in surprise and weathered foreheads are furrowed as they lean forward for a closer look at this remarkable act of Jesus. Thomas's doubt is commonly regarded as something negative—he is often called "Doubting Thomas"—but Jesus invites the doubter in all of us to come and see and touch him. The rest of the people in the room may have had the same doubts before they saw Jesus. They would have had the same questions if they had not been present. Recall the other occasions when Jesus appeared miraculously to the disciples. In Luke's account of another appearance of Jesus (Luke 24:36-53), the others were as disbelieving as Thomas. Just as with Thomas, Jesus had to address their troubled hearts and their doubts. He invited them all to see and to touch his body, and even further he asked for food as proof to them that this was no spirit but a real human body. Even after all this proof, they still could not believe.

Thomas believes but needed to see the wounds for himself. When he returned to the room and heard about Jesus' visit, he needed visible proof. He openly expressed his inner feelings of doubt and was candidly honest about his unbelief. There was no pretence in Thomas, no attempt to spiritualize his response in an effort to be accepted as part of the group. He stood alone in his state of unbelief because he had not seen what the others had seen. Jesus received him exactly where he was, in his present reality.

Jesus also meets us in the questions and doubts of our own life and invites us to trust him completely. Most of us have experienced doubts at some point in our life. Perhaps you know what it feels like to doubt God's existence, or at least God's love and presence. Perhaps you know Thomas's feeling that unless he could see with his own eyes he could not believe. Such times of doubt or dryness of faith are often hard to share because we fear being judged by others or chided for a lack of faith. But doubt that is expressed honestly and openly before God and others leads to greater faith. Perhaps we need to acknowledge that we are more like Thomas than we care to admit, and bring our questions to God so that our faith can be renewed and strengthened.

In a recent period of dryness, I could not sense the presence of Jesus, so my spiritual director suggested that perhaps I should consider this as an invitation to go deeper into my relationship with him. Sensing my desire to have a relationship with Jesus that, like Thomas, was more tangible, she wondered if Jesus could be asking me to walk with him in the darkness rather than seeking to avoid it—to continue with him even if he was leading me to participate in his own suffering. She reminded me that it is in precisely the dark times that Jesus is most present, that he is most real even if I could not see or sense him, because he is our suffering Savior—God with us in every circumstance of life. Following Jesus in the path of unknowing and darkness is not easy, but it draws us quietly into a union with him that is richer and deeper than if we walked only in the sunshine of his presence. In my groping attempts to hold on to Jesus, I often find that rather than grasping him, instead I find myself held, grasped by him and carried by his wounded hands.

For Thomas this experience of having had real, physical contact with Jesus brought him renewed faith and trust. He was drawn into deeper faith and into a closer relationship with his Lord. He was awed by this revelation of the resurrected Jesus and addressed him as "My Lord and my God!" His response was one of awe that he had touched the very person of God. It is not recorded whether or not the other disciples responded with this same affirmation, but Thomas recognized the true nature of Jesus. Thomas's eyes were opened to see Jesus as the eternal One who holds the universe in his hands. These hands continue to extend deep love and compassion because they still bear his wounds. These very wounds assure us that Jesus knows the pain that we experience because he

The Parable of the Blind by Bruegel the Elder

Census at Bethlehem by Bruegel the Elder

Christ in the Wilderness (oil on canvas) by Moretto da Brescia (1498-1554)

The Angelus by Jean-François Millet

The Adoration of the Shepherds by Nicolas Poussin

Christ in the Storm on the Lake of Galilee by Rembrandt van Rijn

The Incredulity of St. Thomas by Michelangelo Merisi da Caravaggio

The Supper at Emmaus by Michelangelo Merisi da Caravaggio

Procession to Calvary by Ridolfo Ghirlandaio

The Visitation by He Qi

The Calling of St. Matthew by Michelangelo Merisi da Caravaggio

The Good Samaritan by Luca Giordano

The Descent from the Cross, central panel of the triptych, by Peter Paul Rubens

has gone down that road already for us. In his painful journey to
the cross, Jesus bore our grief and carried our sorrows. We can
trust that he is with us even when we don't feel his presence. As we
reflect further on how much like Thomas we are, consider the following poem by John Shaw, "Wounded." It is an evocative expression of our own need to have tangible proof that Jesus is with us.

> You could feel its edges,
> You could run your fingers over its red lips
> And probe the hollow like a mouth.
> In a way it had been a thing of beauty;
> the steel, so sharply bright,
> sliding cleanly between the layers,
> slicing the sheets of cells,
> the turfed flesh folding back
> bringing the blinding white and red
> into that land of pulsing gloom.
>
> Thomas, you are like me;
> our faith begins in fingering
> the open wounds.
> It is as if our hopes cannot spring free
> save by permission of those hands,
> that side; as if only after all
> our doubts turn tail—shadows
> before light and blood—
> can the words "My Lord, my God!"
> burst from our mouth
> as wide as wounds.

Jesus said to Thomas, "Blessed are they who did not see, and yet
believed" (John 20:29). He told Thomas that faith goes beyond
anything that he can see or know. He extends the same blessing to
those of us who do not have the advantage of being present at his

postresurrection appearances. We can't see, touch or hear the risen Jesus as these followers do, but we can know his living presence and experience him personally and just as intimately. Dare to be open and honest with your questions and doubts. Come to Jesus with eyes of faith and see his welcome to you. Allow him to draw you closer to himself in love and faith.

FOR REFLECTION AND DISCUSSION

- Return to the story in John's Gospel. Then look again at the painting. How has Caravaggio's meditation on the text enlarged or changed your understanding of this event?

- Enter imaginatively into the painting and notice your response. What emotions do you experience as you place yourself in the painting? Which of the disciples in the painting do you identify with?

- We all experience doubts in our life where we question whether God is really present for us especially in difficult times. What proofs do you demand of Jesus' presence in your own life? What assurances does Jesus offer you?

- Think back to times when you experienced doubts or when you questioned the presence of God. Recall your own struggles to believe. Bring these to Jesus as you meditate on this painting. How does Jesus respond to you? To what part of himself does he draw your hand, heart or mind so that you may touch him?

- Thomas drew back from Jesus in awe at the invitation to see and touch him. What is your response to Jesus' offer of himself to you?

8

RECOGNIZING CHRIST

CARAVAGGIO

The Supper at Emmaus

We have seen up to this point how often all of us fail to recognize God in our midst. In the daily grind of our lives we fail to welcome him because God does not appear to us in ways we expect. John the Baptist told his followers that the Lamb of God was among them, but they did not recognize him: "among you stands One whom you do not know" (John 1:26). Jesus was in their midst, but John was the only one who recognized him for who he really was. As long as we hold certain fixed expectations or ideas of how and where God should be for us, God will always remain hidden from us and will seem silently absent to us.

In chapter six we saw how the openness of the shepherds to having their vision changed led them to recognizing their Messiah. If we were alive at that time in history, would we have recognized Jesus as the Savior of the world? Would we have left our important responsibilities to follow the invitation as unhesitatingly as they did? Most of us would likely say that we would have followed immediately and enthusiastically, and on seeing and worshiping Jesus we would have pledged to live for him. But would we really?

In chapter seven we saw how God desires to be known and to touch us if we would only be attentive, turn and draw near. We saw God taking the initiative through Jesus' incarnation to reach out to us to draw us into a closer relationship with him. The people of John's day needed to have their vision changed in order to see their Messiah in different ways than they had anticipated. They expected a Messiah who would come in power and might to deliver them from their oppressors. Yet here John was telling them that this humble man in ordinary unregal clothing was their King and Deliverer. Their ideas about him needed to be replaced with a new way of seeing. Their eyes required a radical transformation in order to recognize him. As it was in Jesus' day, so it is for us today—we too need to be attentive enough to recognize and respond to God who is among us.

SHARING A MEAL WITH JESUS—LISTENING

One of the most dramatic accounts of transformed seeing presented in Scriptures is found in the familiar story of Jesus appearing to two of his followers on the road to Emmaus after his resurrection. The entire incident is recorded in Luke 24:13-35. Spend some time reading this biblical story contemplatively. Imagine yourself in the scene—listening to the conversation, watching the actions of Jesus and the reactions of the disciples. Engage all of your senses and allow your whole being to be present.

> And behold, two of them were going that very day to a village named Emmaus, which was about seven miles from Jerusalem.

> And they were talking with each other about all these things which had taken place.

> While they were talking and discussing, Jesus Himself approached and began traveling with them.

But their eyes were prevented from recognizing Him.

And He said to them, "What are these words that you are exchanging with one another as you are walking?" And they stood still, looking sad.

One of them, named Cleopas, answered and said to Him, "Are You the only one visiting Jerusalem and unaware of the things which have happened here in these days?"

And He said to them, "What things?" And they said to Him, "The things about Jesus the Nazarene, who was a prophet mighty in deed and word in the sight of God and all the people,

and how the chief priests and our rulers delivered Him to the sentence of death, and crucified Him.

"But we were hoping that it was He who was going to redeem Israel. Indeed, besides all this, it is the third day since these things happened.

"But also some women among us amazed us. When they were at the tomb early in the morning,

and did not find His body, they came, saying that they had also seen a vision of angels who said that He was alive.

"Some of those who were with us went to the tomb and found it just exactly as the women also had said; but Him they did not see."

And He said to them, "O foolish men and slow of heart to believe in all that the prophets have spoken!

"Was it not necessary for the Christ to suffer these things and to enter into His glory?"

Then beginning with Moses and with all the prophets, He explained to them the things concerning Himself in all the Scriptures.

And they approached the village where they were going, and He acted as though He were going farther.

But they urged Him, saying, "Stay with us, for it is getting toward evening, and the day is now nearly over." So He went in to stay with them.

When He had reclined at the table with them, He took the bread and blessed it, and breaking it, He began giving it to them.

Then their eyes were opened and they recognized Him; and He vanished from their sight.

They said to one another, "Were not our hearts burning within us while He was speaking to us on the road, while He was explaining the Scriptures to us?"

And they got up that very hour and returned to Jerusalem, and found gathered together the eleven and those who were with them,

saying, "The Lord has really risen and has appeared to Simon."

They began to relate their experiences on the road and how He was recognized by them in the breaking of the bread.

The story tells of Cleopas and his companion walking on the Emmaus road with a stranger who had joined them. The newcomer was Jesus, but his two friends did not recognize him. As they journeyed, they discussed the events of Jesus' crucifixion, the empty tomb and their hopes for the redemption of Israel. On reaching the village, the stranger accepted their invitation to stay and share a meal with them. At the moment when the visitor blessed the bread and broke it, the eyes of the two disciples were opened. The light of revelation dawned in their sorrowful souls. Their response was amazement, wonder and an immediate return to Jerusalem to announce to the other disciples that Jesus was indeed raised from the dead.

Painting four hundred years ago, Caravaggio used his God-given gift of creative imagination to draw viewers into this event. His depiction invites us to approach the mystery that is God with all of our senses alive and alert to God in our midst. His art emphasized the truth that God can be experienced in the ordinary circumstances of life if we are spiritually attuned with eyes and heart able to see the unseen spiritual realities which surround us. Our common experiences are transformed when we recognize the sacred in the midst of life.

Now take a long and careful look at the painting *Supper at Emmaus* (1601) by Caravaggio.* It hangs in the National Gallery of London and depicts the moment of recognition for the disciples that this is the risen Jesus who shares their meal with them. "When he had reclined at the table with them, He took the bread and blessed it, and breaking it, He began giving it to them. Then their eyes were opened and they recognized Him" (Luke 24:30-31).

THE PAINTING—LOOKING

In Caravaggio's depiction of the story, Jesus sits at a table with his two friends on either side of him. To his right stands a servant or innkeeper. This is an everyday meal with ordinary people. It takes place in an ordinary room of an ordinary house. The scene emerges out of a dark background with the figures placed in the front—an artistic device that forcefully draws us into the picture and immediately engages us in the encounter.

The characters and table setting in this drama are intensified by a light from above. The undisclosed source of this light seems supernatural, almost as if God is actually present at this astounding revelation. The light suggests that something remarkable is taking

---

*On the Internet go to <www.abcgallery.com/C/caravaggio/caravaggio27.html>.

place even though the setting is commonplace. Jesus is no longer dead. He is alive!

At the center of the painting, Jesus leans forward out of the shadows into the light where he is clearly visible. As in his appearance before Thomas, he desires to be seen and known. His left hand hovers in blessing over his own bread, one of the three loaves on the table—one for each of the participants of this meal. His right hand casts a shadow on his left hand of blessing as it reaches out of the painting toward us. It is this action of Jesus' hands that unifies the scene. It is also the action that sparks the startling flash of recognition for the two men.

These followers of Jesus had seen this same familiar gesture during the course of numerous meals shared together, especially at the Last Supper, on the night before Jesus was betrayed. Here we glimpse the archetype of all celebrations of the Eucharist. As his hand stretches out from the shadows to us, Jesus seems to be saying, "I am the bread of life . . . this is my body broken for you . . . do this in remembrance of me." The painting suggests that there are no barriers to this invitation. The table is wide open, Jesus is clearly visible, his welcoming gesture unambiguous in its intention. Yet we are sometimes reluctant to draw near. How often, like Thomas in the previous painting, we physically approach but spiritually hold back parts of ourselves from the full exposure of the Light of the world. Pause for a moment to consider how you respond to Jesus' invitation. What barriers do you erect that keep you from approaching him? In what ways do you avoid entering fully into your shared meals with the Lord?

A CLOSER LOOK

Look for a moment at Jesus' face. How different it is from other depictions of the Messiah before his crucifixion. And it is a different face from the one the disciples remembered. This is a young man's face—full, new and in repose. There is individuality in this face, suggesting that this was a real model used by the artist. It is the face of an ordinary person without any signs of grandeur or heroism. Here is the face of the risen Christ, altered by the resurrection and distinguishable from the Jesus of art history. He looks not at us but down at the bread before him. And yet we are drawn to that face. The light pulls us into the center of the painting toward the person of Jesus. How does this face of Jesus speak to you? What do you read in it—invitation, rejection, scorn, love?

Now notice the response of the two disciples. The one on the right (could this be the impetuous Peter?) flings out his arms in astonishment in a gesture that reminds us of the cross on which Jesus was nailed. It is a gesture that serves to anchor this moment in the painful death that Jesus had undergone. His left arm breaks through the frame of the painting, pushing itself into our viewing space. We cannot ignore or dismiss it because it is thrust directly at us. The man wears a seashell, the symbol of a pilgrim and a reminder of his occupation as a fisherman before he met Jesus. His profile is lit by the same supernatural light which highlights his common, rough features. He is not looking directly at Jesus. Rather, the focus of his attention seems to be the hand of Jesus that is blessing the bread. Again, this underscores the fact that recognition has come through a rather routine action of breaking of bread. The disciple is amazed at the remarkable revelation he is witnessing.

The disciple on the left is also taken aback. He expresses his astonishment by gripping the arms of his chair and pushing himself away from the table. The moment is too stupendous to respond otherwise. His right elbow, emphasized by a small, bright white patch, thrusts itself out at us. The back of his chair gets shoved outside of the frame. You can almost hear the scraping of the chair as it is forcibly pushed backward into our space. Again we are forced to be involved in and to respond to the story—we cannot ignore it. His face, also in profile, is filled with wonder as he too looks at Jesus' hand. Both men's furrowed foreheads shoot upward as their eyes look in incredulity. We can imagine exclamation marks appearing over their heads if this were a cartoon. It *is* Jesus! Christ *is* risen!

One participant in this scene seems to be unaware of the significance of the moment. The servant, not mentioned in the Gospel account, looks at Jesus and does not see the action from either the disciples' point of view or from ours. He misses the significance of the gestures because he was not present at the previous meals with Jesus. He has not known Jesus and has no reminder of familiar gestures to stir him to amazement. Yet he seems to sense something unusual and leans slightly toward Jesus with a hint of interest and questioning on his face. His presence reminds us that at times we are all like this man—not fully involved, mildly curious but uncertain in our response. His shadow on the wall behind Jesus cannot extinguish or mar the brightness of Jesus or the drama of the event. It is all part of the scene. So too is all of our uncertainty, our questioning, our doubts. Jesus appears to hold all of the elements and tensions of light and dark together in his serene presence.

On the table, illuminated by the brilliant white cloth, are the elements of the meal. Every detail is given meticulous attention by the artist because each is significant—the meat, fruit, bread, wine and their respective containers. The basket of fruit, depicted with such realism that they are shown with blemishes and worm holes (the wine that Jesus offers in his blood will never go bad or be corrupted like this fruit), seems to be toppling off the table, and we get a sense of wanting to reach into the painting to save it from falling. The common and ordinary things on this table are made sacred and special by Christ's blessing. This is a miraculously graced moment for the two followers of Jesus.

Follow the movement made by the white highlights and by the faces in the painting. See how they cause our eyes to move in a unified rhythm from Jesus' face, down his left arm to the face and arms of the man on the right, across the white tablecloth, to the white spot on the sleeve of the disciple on the left, upward to the white armband and that of the servant and back to Jesus. Together with the gestures of all three main characters and the precariously placed fruit basket, they command our attention, pulling us into the scene, and almost force us to make some response to this event. Held together by the figure of Jesus in the middle of the painting, these things focus our attention and compel us to look closely at what this painting is calling us to.

JESUS' INVITATION—RESPONDING

We are invited to share not only in the revelation but also in the meal. The empty place at the table is open wide enough for us to pull up a chair and join in this meal. Jesus' outstretched hand, pointing directly at us, extends an invitation to each one of us. Consider how your participation in the Lord's Supper can be transformed by the truths presented here. How real is the presence of Jesus at the Communion Table? Does this reality cause you to respond with joyful wonder and praise?

Caravaggio's painting opens a window for us to experience the presence of the risen Christ. As you reflect further on the biblical text and on the painting, consider the ways you experience the presence of God in the everyday circumstances of your life. Approach all of life's experiences with gratitude and joy because God is in each one of them.

FOR REFLECTION AND DISCUSSION

- As you reflect further on the text and painting, you may want to take some time to review your day. Where was God in it? At what times and places did you recognize God's presence and action? In hindsight, where were you unaware of God's presence? Where did you fail to recognize God? In what ways can you be more open to recognizing Jesus through your day?

- How has Jesus been present to you in the ordinary events of your life? How aware were you of those moments? How have you responded? Luke's account describes the disciples shown here as rushing off to tell the others about this encounter. They do not keep it to themselves. In what ways has your response been like or unlike that of these two followers of Jesus?

- The men in this story respond as little children—unselfconsciously, spontaneously and with undiluted amazement. What role does wonder play in your faith journey? If none at all, pray that your eyes might be opened and your vision transformed so that you might see the presence of the wondrous in all of life.

Part Three

TRANSFORMED LIVING

9

THE WAY OF THE CROSS

Ridolfo Ghirlandaio
Procession to Calvary

hat connects all the participants in the stories of the previous section is their awakening to God and their subsequent response. Each one responded to Jesus' invitations to see what he saw and learn how he saw, but also to participate in his life. This involved a change in how they lived—seeing with new eyes, they experienced a new life. They came to see things as they really are—as God sees them. This led to a life where Jesus took his place on the throne of their heart. They were transformed not only in their vision but in their lives. When God becomes the center of our life, we become aware that God's creative love is within us. This enables us to live in freedom, with authenticity and with a new awareness of what truly is and is important.

An aria from Bach's *St. Matthew Passion* expresses this transformation beautifully. Loosely translated from the original German, it reads: "Purify yourself, my heart, I myself will bury Jesus. For he shall henceforth evermore sweetly take his rest in me. World, get out, let Jesus in!" This journey of awareness has been taking us into the heart of Jesus himself as continuously we surrender more and more of ourselves to him. Gradually we begin to resemble Jesus in his love, compassion and full embrace of life. We slowly take on the mind and heart of God.

Human beings long for connectedness to their Creator. As Augustine's familiar words remind us: "Our hearts are restless until they find their rest in Thee." Remarkably, however, God's longing for us is even greater than ours for him. Having created us for himself and for his pleasure, God constantly seeks us out. God initiates our yearning, willing "that we should push on into His presence and live our whole life there."

Our spiritual journey is our return to our true home. Where we once enjoyed unbroken fellowship with God in a garden of beauty and tranquility, we now struggle against the weeds and thorns that block our path back to the divine. The prayer of Richard of Chichester expresses this quest simply but profoundly: "May I know Thee more clearly, love Thee more dearly, follow Thee more nearly, day by day."

Christian transformation is a journey in which our eyes, heart and life are gradually purified until we see God face to face. It is movement toward God that involves allowing God to change our heart and ultimately our ways of living. In *Pilgrim's Progress*, John Bunyan envisions it as wrestling with the obstacles that prevent our progress toward God. He describes it as a way to glory where pilgrims must relinquish their burdens and die to the things that keep them from seeing the face of God. With clearer vision and a heightened awareness of God's presence in the midst of our work and life, how then are we to live? We have only to look at Jesus and how he lived out his life on the earth to discover the pattern for our own lives.

As we meditate on Jesus' life, we see how his journey models the way for us to face the challenges and joys of our journey and be fully surrendered to God—how to die to self and allow God to have complete rule in our heart. Jesus never lost sight of the destination of his journey. He was entirely focused on doing God's will. His vision was never clouded by distractions or by his own selfish desires. He followed his Father's leading, trusting that God was always with him, even in the most difficult stages of his journey.

Jesus' life was animated by deep involvement in the lives of the people who surrounded him. He experienced joyful times of celebration, sad times of losing people he loved, highly emotional occasions of being revered and reviled, lonely and misunderstood times, and times of frustration and anger. His darkest moments, of course, were those which led up to his prayerful struggle in Gethsemane, his arrest and trial, and his subsequent death on a cross. Forced to carry his own cross on the way to his crucifixion, Jesus was subjected to scorn, ridicule and agony.

LISTENING

The artist Ridolfo Ghirlandaio has based his work on the text "They took Jesus, therefore, and He went out, bearing His own cross, to the place called the Place of a Skull, which is called in Hebrew, Golgotha" (John 19:17). In his painting titled *Procession to Calvary*, we see Jesus carrying his cross toward the hill of Golgotha, surrounded by some of his closest followers as well as soldiers and others on horseback and on foot.

Take a few minutes in silence and stillness to slowly and prayerfully read John 19:16-18, as well as Luke 23:26-32 for a fuller account. Notice anything that holds your attention. Pause and reflect on any images, memories or associations that may come to you.

So he then handed Him over to them to be crucified.

They took Jesus, therefore, and He went out, bearing His own cross, to the place called the Place of a Skull, which is called in Hebrew, Golgotha.

Ridolfo Ghirlandaio (1483-1561)

Ghirlandaio lived and worked in Italy during the High Renaissance. During this period the world witnessed the flourishing of its greatest artists—Raphael, Michelangelo and Da Vinci—all of whom greatly influenced Ghirlandaio. Known mostly for his portraits, he learned his craft as a young boy from his father. When he was eleven years old, his father died and he went to live with his uncle who was also an artist. As was the case for most artists in this period of history, he would have known the Bible stories well. His commissioned works were mostly altarpieces and frescoes for churches, and portraits. *Procession to Calvary* (1505) was one of his earliest commissions. It was produced as an altarpiece for the church of San Gallo in Florence and is now on display at the National Gallery of Art, London.

There they crucified Him, and with Him two other men, one on either side, and Jesus in between.

Now take some time for a long, slow look at this painting.* What immediately draws your interest? Who or what is the focus here? How do you respond to it?

THE PAINTING—LOOKING

The painting depicts three stages of a pathway in which different groups of people are traveling to the same destination. It is the path that Jesus has taken and which leads toward his place of crucifixion. Behind is a group that follows Jesus toward Gol-

---

*On the Internet go to <www.nationalgallery.org.uk/upload/img/ghirlandaio-proces sion-calvary-NG1143-fm.jpg>.

gotha. Ahead of him is another group that winds its way closer to the site.

First, look at the path along which Jesus makes his way. In the right corner of the painting a procession of noblemen emerges from a grand city, making their way toward the final destination where momentous events are about to unfold. They seem unaware of the earth-shattering events about to take place ahead of them. They travel along, casually pausing to chat and confer with each other— just another outing, just another spectacle to witness.

Their path takes them away from the prosperous city behind them, through an archway that is crumbling into ruin. This decaying arch marks the beginning of the way of suffering and death as it leads forward and upward toward the hill of the skull. Close to this curved opening is a barren, eroded rock to which a lone, scrubby tree and a dead brown root cling. This provides a sharp contrast to the rich and peaceful urban setting that lies behind, as well as a foreshadowing of the stark tree on which Jesus is to be hung. The participants in this part of the scene know where this road leads, although they have no understanding of its weighty significance. They follow, full of curiosity and interest.

In the opposite, left corner of the painting, we see others farther along on the trail up toward the hill. The figures are less distinct, but they appear to be the parties accompanying the two thieves who are to be crucified with Jesus on this fateful day. Following this path upward we arrive at the hill itself, already prepared for the two thieves. Two crosses, already anchored to their spot, loom into the sky which is beginning to darken with gathering clouds. Almost at the center of this distant hill, a horseman carries a tall red standard that pierces the center of the hill, marking the exact place where Jesus' cross will be placed. The short, horizontal beam of the cross and the long, aggressive spear at the center of the painting intersect to form a triangle that accentuates Jesus' place of crucifixion. Jesus himself is placed directly in line with this to leave no question for the viewer where he is headed. Nor does it leave any question about his fate. The soft, gentle colors of the background of the painting belie the ugliness and suffering of what is taking place directly in front of us.

The two groups on either side of the painting frame the central figure of Jesus and help focus our attention on him. Once announced by rejoicing angels and received with worship and adoration by shepherds and kings, Jesus is now rejected and despised. Growing opposition and demand for his death by his detractors has led to this cruel end. Here he walks painfully and slowly toward his dark and final hours on earth.

We may have some trouble seeing the details in this painting, and it may be helpful to use a larger image or a magnifying glass, but let's now look more closely at the figure of Jesus. He stands out in his red robe, his body bent under the weight of the cross as he walks barefoot on the stony path. He is also being dragged along by a rope tied to his waist, which the soldier ahead of him firmly grips. In spite of his suffering and anguish, Jesus' face appears calm and tranquil. The crown of thorns presses heavily on his head. From it drops of blood stream down his brow and his neck. Yet he presses on toward his goal, fully accepting his Father's will. His struggle in the garden of Gethsemane is over, and now we see him in serene and complete submission to his calling.

As Jesus bears his cross with courage and faith, would he have had trouble finding God in the midst of this situation? Or was he so intent on pleasing his Father that his inner focus was on his Father from whom he always drew strength and resolve? Jesus voluntarily and willingly humbled himself to identify fully with humankind. He stooped so low that he subjected himself to death on a cross. How can Jesus' attitude of dependence on God be helpful for us as we look for his presence among all of life's circumstances?

A MOMENT ON THE JOURNEY

Ghirlandaio's visual representation of Jesus' journey to Calvary depicts him being followed by "a large crowd of people, and of women who were mourning and lamenting Him" (Luke 23:27). Here we see the small band of devoted followers very close to Jesus, their golden haloes distinguishing them from the others. They accompany him on his painful route to Calvary. They are conformed to his suffering as they walk with him and enter into his painful struggle. They are entirely focused on him as they walk closely behind. Their faces are mournful, yet they bear an incredible stillness and peace about them—a peace that stands in bold contrast to the other people in the scene. They display an inner serenity that contradicts their outer circumstances.

Also note the similarity between their posture and faces and that of Jesus. As his body stoops under the weight of the cross, so these women lean toward Jesus with their gazes fixed on him. John, the beloved disciple, robed in red and gazing almost blissfully toward heaven, stands close to the mother of Jesus. We anticipate that moment when Jesus, hanging from the cross, connects Mary and John, saying, "'Woman, behold your son!' Then He said to the disciple, 'Behold, your mother!'" (John 19:26-27). The followers of Jesus are beginning to resemble him not only in his suffering but in his serenity and trust in the Father. The inner transformation that began from the times of intimacy spent with Jesus is becoming evident in their lives, visible on the outside.

The groups of opposing forces surrounding Jesus appear antagonistic and harsh. The anger and hostility on their faces stand in sharp contrast to the gentle faces of those who are Jesus' friends. Depicted mostly in profile, their features are crisply defined and hard. Notice the aggressive face of the man on the extreme left and the clenched fist of another behind him. Look at the soldier immediately in front of the horse. He shows a face full of rage and hatred as he looks toward the women. All of this is emphasized by the sharp angular diagonals of the cross and lance in the middle of the painting. The hard, brightly metallic armor of the mounted soldier, the sharp edges of helmets and weapons emphasize their animosity.

Go back and look again at the faces of all the people in the painting. What is unusual about them?

Notice that almost all are looking somewhere other than outward to the viewer. There are actually only two faces that look directly at us. First, there is the man on the far left carrying a long rifle. He looks unwaveringly at us as he points his thumb back toward the figure of Jesus. There is also the face that looks at us on the cloth held by the woman who kneels slightly behind Jesus. Historically identified by Roman Catholics as Veronica, she has used it to wipe the sweat and blood from the face of Jesus. This action has imprinted Jesus' face on the cloth, and now Jesus' own face seems to be gazing out at us. Both these faces confront us with questions about our own journey of transformation.

WHO DO YOU SAY THAT I AM?—RESPONDING

In Matthew 16:15 Jesus asks his disciples, "Who do you say that I am?" The gesture of this man who faces us confronts us with the same question. What do we make of this suffering Savior? What is our response? Is it one of recognition that this is truly the Christ, the Son of God and Savior of the world? Will we join his friends and follow too, even if the way is temporarily dark and unattractive? Do we recognize Jesus as the redeemer of our souls?

The question is addressed to us again from the face that we encounter on the cloth. The woman who holds it does so tenderly. She expresses in visible form the mystery of the incarnation. A verse of the Christmas carol "O Little Town of Bethlehem" prays that the holy child of Bethlehem would "be born in us today." We are invited to receive Jesus' own presence, as symbolized in this imprinted image, into ourselves. We are invited to bear his image—not on a cloth but in our very being. Like the woman who holds this sacred cloth, we too come to bear his image by being intimately connected to him. Notice how her hands touch his as she takes the cloth from Jesus. In his life, death and resurrection, he asks us to come near and touch him for our healing and salvation. Are we close enough to meet Jesus in the intimacy he longs to share with us?

Look again at the company of Jesus' friends. They huddle close to him, refusing to be separated from him no matter where his path leads. Their physical connectedness in the scene expresses the spiritual intimacy they share with him. They are also connected by the same kind of clothing, their serene demeanors and their obvious devotion to Jesus. Notice that except for the kneeling woman, all follow Jesus with empty hands. They represent pilgrims who are spiritually receptive to becoming more closely intimate with their Lord. They have given up all to follow him. They remind us of Jesus' teaching that "if anyone wishes to come after Me, he must deny himself, and take up his cross and follow Me" (Matthew 16:24).

These followers have journeyed with Jesus and now dare to risk being publicly identified with him. They are united with their Lord, even in his suffering. Sharing our faith journey with others creates the kind of community that Jesus encouraged and modeled in his relationships with his disciples. It is here that we find strength as we journey together. It is here that we help each other to see where he is in the middle of life's adversities.

GETTING PERSONAL

Ghirlandaio's painting invites us to stay close to Jesus as we follow him. It invites us to a place of surrender where we can be shaped into the image of God's Son. It encourages us to be conformed to the image of Christ—to become more and more like him in his life and in his death.

Bearing my cross is not an attractive thought, but I like to think of myself as one among those who were following close behind Jesus on his way to Golgotha. I am struck by how physically connected the women are to Jesus in his suffering. I may not be as brave or as resolute as the women in the painting, but I feel drawn to joining them so that I too can be close to my Lord.

In his book *Long on the Journey*, Basil Pennington states that our struggles and suffering are given perspective and meaning when we walk "the Way of the Cross." This is so is because "at the end there is always ultimate meaning, the empty tomb—resurrection and ascension—for Christ and for each one of us, his members." He goes on:

> We are on a journey, and like any journey, it would be meaningless if it did not have a destination. But it does have a destination, a wonderful, glorious, assured destination. The way thereto has been opened to us by this sorrowful journey to Calvary; it has been assured to us by this journey. The Way of the Cross underlines the meaning of all life, even as it gives meaning to the little—and the greater—sufferings and crosses of life.

Allow yourself to be drawn closer to Jesus and to follow him with devotion and surrender as he leads you to the ultimate destination—transformation and union with God. Let the one who is the Way lead you on the only journey worth pursuing.

ↀ

FOR REFLECTION AND DISCUSSION

- The artist presents the journey of following Jesus as identifying with him in his suffering. Paul exhorts us to rejoice in the Lord (Philippians 3:1), but he connects this to knowing the "fellowship of His sufferings, being conformed to His death; in order that I may attain to the resurrection from the dead" (Philippians 3:10-11). How do you identify with Jesus in his suffering?

- Take a moment and place yourself within the painting. Where are you in relation to Jesus as he makes this journey to Calvary? Are you in the distance, far from him, or are you close enough to touch him?

- Scripture reminds us to keep our eyes fixed on Jesus. As you enter into the painting with your imagination and senses alert, where are your eyes focused—downward with despair or upward toward Jesus' face with hope and trust?

- Jesus created a close-knit community of followers bound strongly together in love. They found encouragement for their faith and strength in their time of sorrow by drawing together. With which group in the painting do you most identify at this point in your own journey? How has your own faith community held and supported you on your journey toward transformation?

10

CALLED TO FOLLOW

CARAVAGGIO
The Calling of St. Matthew

*T*he Christian spiritual journey is a response to God's invitation to allow grace to transform us. Our heart can only be transformed through the grace and love of God. Such love is always offered to us but we have to receive it and allow it to change us. We must be willing to relinquish our self-centered ways of being and let God be the center of our life. Following the way of Christ, we live the Christian mystery and increasingly reflect the image of God. The beginning of this journey is an encounter with the living God, which may be sudden or gradual. However it happens, it will always involve a turning or a change of direction and an awakening. The Bible records many conversions or awakenings where God is met in a spectacular way. Generally, however, most involve a non-dramatic first encounter and recurring acts of turning.

Turning toward God makes sense because God is the one who has made the first move in turning toward us. God always takes the initiative—God first notices us, lays eyes of love on us, calls us by name and invites us to join in the fellowship of the Trinity. Our response to this invitation will be but a first step on a lifelong transformational journey of awakening and coming to know God experientially. It is a journey of becoming our true self in Christ— a journey where we grow into Christlikeness.

THE CALL OF ST. MATTHEW—LISTENING

Matthew's first encounter with Jesus is a story that tells us about his response to Jesus' love. The account of his call is recorded in three of the Gospels. Matthew and Mark describe this event in concise, direct language. There are no elaborations, no added details, simply stating that Matthew rose and followed. Luke's description is similarly plain but adds that Matthew left everything behind and immediately followed Jesus.

Take some time to read the story as it is recorded in Luke 5:27-32. Allow yourself to daydream as you read it, placing yourself imaginatively in the scene. Be there in the scene and experience it with all of your senses fully alert. Note what is happening—attend to sounds, smells, sights, actions.

> After that He went out and noticed a tax collector named Levi sitting in the tax booth, and He said to him, "Follow Me."
>
> And he left everything behind, and got up and began to follow Him.
>
> And Levi gave a big reception for Him in his house; and there was a great crowd of tax collectors and other people who were reclining at the table with them.
>
> The Pharisees and their scribes began grumbling at His disciples, saying, "Why do you eat and drink with the tax collectors and sinners?"
>
> And Jesus answered and said to them, "It is not those who are well who need a physician, but those who are sick.
>
> "I have not come to call the righteous but sinners to repentance."

CARAVAGGIO'S MEDITATION—LOOKING

Now take some time to look carefully at *The Calling of St. Matthew* by Caravaggio.* This painting is Caravaggio's meditation on the simple story of a man called Levi sitting in his tax office while Jesus passes by, sees him and calls him to follow. As the focus for his work, the artist chooses the verses, "And after that He went out and noticed a tax collector named Levi sitting in the tax booth, and He said to him, 'Follow Me.' And he left everything behind, and got up and began to follow Him" (Luke 5:27-28).

The Calling of St. Matthew was Caravaggio's first commissioned painting, and occupies an entire wall of the Contarelli Chapel in Rome. It measures ten-and-a-half feet by eleven feet. The other two walls of the chapel depict scenes of Matthew writing his Gospel, and his martyrdom. The works are large, with life-size figures. They fill the small chapel they are housed in and captivate one's attention. They powerfully engage the viewer with the force of their incredible realism and with the artist's dramatic juxtaposition of light and dark.

Seeing the original of this painting for the first time in the Contarelli Chapel in Rome, I was moved to tears and riveted by its power. The size of the figures and the prominence of Jesus' hand in the center gripped my attention. That hand seemed to be pointing at me and inviting me to turn and follow Jesus. Matthew's finger pointing to himself could have been my own, questioning my worthiness to be chosen and called to follow. It was easy for me to place myself in the painting and *be* Matthew, responding to Jesus' invitation with amazement. And I marveled again at God's reckless love for me.

Caravaggio's interpretation of this story is rich and poignant, the details he includes being full of profound spiritual significance. A close look and further meditation on the painting will enlarge

*On the Internet go to <www.abcgallery.com/C/caravaggio/caravaggio24.html>.

our understanding of the story and of the transformational journey. What do you notice when you look at this painting? What questions does it ask of you? How do you respond?

Unlike many of our preconceived images of this scene, Caravaggio places the action indoors and within his own time and place. The painting is divided into two unequal halves. The left half is contained within a horizontal rectangle while the right is held in a vertical one. Both are bridged and unified by Jesus' outstretched hand, which reaches across the space between them. On the left is a group of five men seated at a table dressed in the contemporary European style of Caravaggio's time. On the right are two other men, one of them Jesus, who enter the darkened room. They are clothed in the attire of Jesus' day. I will return to the significance of this later. Above them, forming the dividing line between the two halves, is a large, prominent window. Slicing diagonally and dramatically across the canvas is a powerful beam of light that illuminates the faces and figures of those at the table. The figures in the painting show us different ways of responding to this call to transformation.

As you look at the painting, what is the first thing that catches your eye? Perhaps it is the beam of light, or maybe it is Jesus' hand, the window, the group of men at the table on the left, or the two men on the right of the painting. Whatever it is, pause for a moment to look and reflect, and then see where this first impression takes you. (Sometimes using a magnifying glass to really look at the painting is helpful.)

The dramatic use of light and dark—known as *chiaroscuro*—was more than just an artistic technique for Caravaggio. He used it to convey spiritual truths that speak of interior spiritual darkness and inner light. Notice that the scene takes place in a darkened room. The light that enters does not come from the window but from some source outside—an indication that this is not any ordinary light. It is the supernatural light of God's very presence. This is a moment of tremendous spiritual significance. It is a moment of transformation. The light pierces the darkness of the room and illuminates the faces of the people around the table.

WHO, ME?

Let's look more carefully at this left side of the painting. Recall what had happened before this moment. Jesus had noticed the tax collector and had called out to him to follow. Here, Matthew sits with four other people. His right hand is suspended over the table as he holds some of the money that is being counted. He is recording his day's take. With his left hand, he points to himself with his index finger. Or perhaps it points to the two persons on his right, who are leaning over the table. Matthew may be wondering if Jesus really means him or these two beside him. He seems to be astonished that God's light and love would rest on him, and we can almost hear him asking the question, "Who, me?"

Remember who Matthew was—a tax collector, a person regarded as a cheat, who would skim off tax money for his own gain. He was an outcast in his culture and relegated to the edges of society along with lepers and prostitutes—unloved, unlovely and unwholesome. Yet here he was with his friends being invited to follow Jesus. He is being offered a chance to find a new identity as one who is beloved in Christ. He is being called to a journey where his heart and life would be transformed—where his life would be completely turned around.

Matthew's questioning face, entirely lit by the holy light, looks toward Jesus. His gaze is direct and open. The objects of Matthew's focus and attention are Jesus and his voice. The outstretched hand of Jesus just below the window, emphasized by a red sleeve, is also lit by that light. It is a commanding presence that summons Matthew to a new life where he is loved and accepted just as he is.

Jesus may have passed by the tax office often and seen Matthew at his work, maybe even have known him by name. He definitely would have known how totally unacceptable he was in his society. Yet he does the extraordinary in breaking from his cultural tradition. He ignores the conventions of his day that demand avoidance of people such as Matthew. He simply calls him and invites him to follow. If you look closely, you may see that Jesus' feet are already turned in the direction that will take him out of the room and toward a different path.

At the frozen moment captured in this painting, Matthew has not yet obeyed that call. He has just heard Jesus calling his name and inviting him to follow. It is a moment of decision as he sits in the glare of light that shows him for who he really is. It is a light that exposes his weaknesses and sin. The darkness of the room, which symbolizes the internal darkness of Matthew's soul, is pierced by the light of holy presence. His soul is laid bare by the brightness of glory. He comes face to face with himself and with Jesus, and now must make the choice to follow or not.

Switch your attention for a moment to the right side of the painting. Jesus stands with Peter, who has already been called and has decided to follow. The artist places him in the darkest side of the painting and behind the disciple. He is not easy to find in the darkness. There is a faint halo around his head to ensure that we do not miss who he is. His hand reaches out from the darkness and points authoritatively and decisively toward Matthew. Yet it is also a gentle hand—a hand that is offering life and forgiveness. It is an inviting hand. Jesus never calls us coercively, or with force. His face in the half-light looks at the tax collector with compassion and love.

Matthew begins to know what unconditional love is through Jesus' acceptance of him in his present condition. He knows how greedy and duplicitous his heart has been in the way he lived and the way he has earned his living. He seems to be aware of his need for transformation. Perhaps he begins to realize that his self-worth really comes from a life lived in dependence on God. Now love and life are offered to him without any questions asked. He is being offered unconditional love, freedom and an opportunity to become a new person. He is being summoned to fix his eyes on Jesus rather than on earthly treasure. He is being asked to move from darkness into the light of God's love. This love is the only thing that can bring transformation.

My poet friend from New Zealand, Kathy Hughes, expresses well in "Love with No Edges" what Matthew must have experienced in his call to light and life.

> Love given free of charge,
> no strings attached, no puppets.
>
> Acceptance as is,
> no judgment, no prosecution.
>
> Love with no edges,
> a wide open plain.
>
> No accusations
> to knock me down.
>
> Just love warmly leading into the sun
> to freedom, laughter and life.

But what if Matthew had ignored or missed the voice of Jesus? What if he had not looked at Jesus or had ignored him when he was addressed? What if he had chosen to remain in the darkness of that stuffy room? Notice the two figures at the furthest left of the painting. One sits totally engrossed in something on the table. If we look really closely we see that he is counting some coins on the table. On the table we see also a pen in an inkwell and a ledger for recording the day's payments. Another man leans over this seated figure as he adjusts his spectacles to get a closer look at the profits. He seems to be the oldest in the group. Both are so absorbed in their business that they don't even notice that Jesus has entered the room. They seem oblivious to the invitation offered to Matthew.

With eyes focused on more earthly things, they miss Jesus entirely and miss their opportunity to also be invited to new life in Christ.

The two younger men on Matthew's left are curious at this interruption in their affairs. One leans forward and seems to be engaged in conversation with Peter. The youngest one leans on Matthew and appears hesitant, looking dubiously on, seeming to pull back slightly from the pair who have entered his space, unsure of what this encounter may mean for him. He and his companion on the bench notice the cause of this interruption, become interested and begin to be engaged. The choice is offered to them too through the invitation of the disciple whose hand is similarly stretched out to them. The one with his back to us sits straddled on a bench with his sword diagonally pointing toward Matthew—another way to identify Matthew in the painting. Could his posture indicate that he is interested enough that he is about to make a decision? One hand rests on the table while the other is on the bench, which makes him appear to be getting ready to rise up and follow. He straddles the familiar world that he shares with the others in the scene and the unknown future that is being offered to him. His decision has yet to be determined.

Notice that the five men at the table are of different ages. They range clockwise from a very young boy who leans on Matthew, to a slightly older one who straddles the bench, to a young adult counting the money, to the oldest one with the spectacles, and finally to Matthew himself, who seems to be a mature adult. The invitation is offered to everyone, no matter how old. Jesus' hand, frozen here in space, commands attention and calls to people of all ages. The invitation to a love relationship with Jesus is extended to everyone.

Note the differences in the clothing between the two groups of people. On the left, colors, textures and ornamentation all point to a world that is rich and sumptuous. Look at Caravaggio's masterly handling of feathers, silks, satins, fur and velvets as the miraculous light plays on the whole scene, highlighting the folds and drapery of luxurious fabrics, and the textures of metal and wood. On the right, Jesus and Peter are dressed in plain, unadorned Palestinian clothing—a sharp contrast to that of the seated group. This contrast underscores the fact that Jesus spans all time and all ages to call people to follow him. Jesus did not come just to call those of his own period in history but all people across all time.

THE CALL AND THE CROSS—RESPONDING

But what exactly does this invitation entail? We get a clue from the window that takes up such a large space in the painting. The panes form an obvious cross, and Caravaggio places Jesus' hand immediately below it. We remember Jesus' words that we must deny ourselves, take up our cross and follow him. As Jesus took up his cross, which led to Calvary, so too must we take up our own cross and die to self. This means awakening to Jesus' invitation, leaving behind the life we once led, turning away from our old ways of being and following Jesus' way. It involves a turning from something and toward a new orientation. For Matthew, it meant leaving behind his wealth, his former familiar ways of being, his fine clothing and his rich life. To follow Jesus would have meant taking on the simple life that Jesus offered to all his followers. In Caravaggio's time this was also a call to take up vows of poverty—a practice that reflected the ideals of the church of his day.

Those who had already decided to follow Jesus had given up their livelihoods and joined Jesus in a life of simplicity. The disciple in the painting, traditionally identified as Peter, draws our attention to this aspect as he leans forward in order to invite others to join in the journey. Peter, like Jesus, is barefooted and plainly dressed. He has no obvious wealth, only a staff and cloak. He has abandoned his former life as a fisherman and given up everything to follow. Look at how similar his hand is to Jesus' hand. He is imitating Jesus by gently reaching out, by engaging others in conversation and by inviting them to follow as well. He is gradually becoming more Christlike as he keeps his eyes and life focused on Jesus.

As represented by Caravaggio, the call of Jesus comes to us in the midst of the ordinary and everyday activities of life. Sometimes our daily experience is dark and burdensome. Yet the light of God is always present, piercing the gloom of our earthly struggles. Jesus continually enters into every experience of our life with his hand outstretched and invites us to turn to him. His presence is sometimes difficult to discern, but if we practice being aware, awake and attentive, we will know that he has entered our room and called us by name. Then we can turn and respond with a resounding yes to his love and light.

We know Matthew's response. He immediately got up, left everything behind and followed Jesus. Later on in Luke 5 we learn that he had a dinner at his house where guests included not only Jesus but others who were also tax collectors. He had given everything to be a disciple of Jesus and began to call others to transformation. That too is part of the journey.

The final stage on this transformational journey is wonderfully expressed in Charles Wesley's well-known hymn "Love Divine, All Loves Excelling" (1747):

> Finish, then, thy new creation;
> pure and spotless let us be.
> Let us see thy great salvation
> perfectly restored in thee;
> Changed from glory into glory,
> till in heaven we take our place,
> Till we cast our crowns before thee,
> lost in wonder, love and praise.

Allow God to do the work of transformation as you walk through each day. Treat every welcome or unwelcome interruption as an opportunity to know God's presence and turn to life and love. Become more attentive to the ongoing call of Jesus in your life. Allow yourself to respond to the wonder of his transforming love. Journey in this love and be changed from glory into glory until God completes the divine work of restoration and reformation.

FOR REFLECTION AND DISCUSSION

- Spend some time looking again at the painting. What has changed for you? What do you see differently?

- In your imagination take a step into the painting and try to identify with each of the characters. There is a space at the table for you too. What would you be preoccupied with when Jesus enters your dark room? Where is your focus? What is on your table in front of you that engrosses you? Do you even notice when Jesus enters?

- What is it like to have the full force of the light of God shine on you? What does this light expose in your life that you need to surrender to God? How does this light enable you to see yourself and everything in a new way? What would you have to abandon in order to more fully follow Jesus?

- What is it like to hear the voice of Jesus calling you to be with him and to journey more intimately with him?

- What keeps you from making a decision to follow as you "straddle the bench"? What attracts or repels you about Jesus' call? What causes you to hesitate and pull back into the shadows?

- How aware are you of Jesus' voice and presence in the midst of your present life experiences—calling you to turn and be transformed? How do you respond?

11

SEEING CHRIST
IN OTHERS

HE QI
The Visitation

*H*earts that are truly transformed by the love of God become places that offer space for hospitality to others—not just to those within our own faith community but to all people. This broad view of hospitality was central to the ancient practices of Jewish culture and Christian monasticism. Think of the many stories in the Bible where visitors are received openly with footwashing and a meal. The story of Abraham offering welcome to three strangers comes immediately to mind. The Rule of St. Benedict (chap. 53, v. 1) encourages its adherents to let all guests who arrive, whether a stranger or not, be received like Christ. They do this because Jesus will say to them when they see him in heaven that they received him when he came as a guest among them. Emulating Jesus' own inclusion of every person he met, we are to extend love and grace to everyone. We mediate grace to others when we receive all guests into our heart as Christ.

The gift of hospitality, offered in love to all people, begins with a heart that has been transformed by love. From here, and with the inner stillness which comes from contemplative prayer, we are enabled to set aside our own preoccupations and interests in order to be fully present to another. Having practiced attentiveness to God in stillness we can now be personally and fully attentive to others. The space we offer is sacred space because God is there and is the true host. We honor the mystical presence of Christ in each person when we welcome and embrace them as Christ.

We are meant to make the spiritual journey with others. The experience of God cries out within us to be shared, and doing so with wise, trusted companions is an important part of the way we learn to attend to the movement of the Spirit in daily life. This is the kind of sharing that lies at the heart of spiritual companionship. It can be expressed simply as guest friendship or, more intentionally and formally, in spiritual direction. In both ways we share our experience of God and learn to discern the action of God in our life. We focus on the mystery that connects us to each other and to God.

MARY VISITS ELIZABETH—LISTENING

Luke tells us that when Mary heard that she would be the mother of the Messiah she hurried to her cousin's house to share the news. Elizabeth, who herself had been miraculously blessed by the Lord, greeted Mary with openness and warmth. We do not know the details of what they said to each other. But we see enough of their interaction to be able to identify a number of important elements that stretch our view of what soul hospitality looks like. These we will explore as we look at this work of art together.

But first, take some time to reflectively read the entire story in Luke 1:39-56. Sit with the images as they come into your mind. You may even have a mental picture that emerges from your memories of a favorite Christmas card, some other painting or even a staged presentation. Attend to the scene and be present there to see what is happening. Listen in on the conversation and see if you can get a sense of the mood of the visit.

Now at this time Mary arose and went in a hurry to the hill country, to a city of Judah,

and entered the house of Zacharias and greeted Elizabeth.

When Elizabeth heard Mary's greeting, the baby leaped in her womb; and Elizabeth was filled with the Holy Spirit.

And she cried out with a loud voice and said, "Blessed are you among women, and blessed is the fruit of your womb!

"And how has it happened to me, that the mother of my Lord would come to me?

"For behold, when the sound of your greeting reached my ears, the baby leaped in my womb for joy.

"And blessed is she who believed that there would be a fulfillment of what had been spoken to her by the Lord."

And Mary said:

"My soul exalts the Lord,
And my spirit has rejoiced in God my Savior.
"For He has had regard for the humble state of His
    bondslave;
For behold, from this time on all generations will count
    me blessed.
"For the Mighty One has done great things for me;
And holy is His name.
"AND HIS MERCY IS UPON GENERATION AFTER GENERATION
    TOWARD THOSE WHO FEAR HIM.
"He has done mighty deeds with His arm;
He has scattered those who were proud in the thoughts
    of their heart.

"He has brought down rulers from their thrones,
And has exalted those who were humble.
"HE HAS FILLED THE HUNGRY WITH GOOD THINGS;
And sent away the rich empty-handed.
"He has given help to Israel His servant,
In remembrance of His mercy,
As He spoke to our fathers,
To Abraham and his descendants forever."

And Mary stayed with her about three months, and then returned to her home.

Then bring these imaginative insights with you as you approach He Qi's depiction of this important biblical event. The artist bases his painting on the text "when Elizabeth heard Mary's greeting, the baby leaped in her womb; and Elizabeth was filled with the Holy Spirit" (Luke 1:41). His painting is called *The Visitation*.

Looking at *The Visitation*, you will immediately be struck by the artist's bold lines and bright colors.* He Qi combines painting techniques from traditional Chinese folk art and Western classical art to produce paintings that are almost iconic in their representation. Its simplicity and power reaches people of all cultures and nationalities. Allow this painting to speak new meanings to you. What do you see? What do you hear or sense as you first look at it? How does this painting change your own mental picture of this story?

The account in Luke tells us that after the angel Gabriel appeared to Mary, she immediately went to her cousin Elizabeth to tell her what happened. On hearing Mary's greeting the miraculous child in Elizabeth's own womb leaped, and Elizabeth experienced an infilling of the Holy Spirit. She then proclaimed the blessedness of Mary's faith in God's promises, affirming her cousin as

---

*On the Internet go to <www.heqigallery.com/shop/40-The-Visitation.jpg>.

He Qi

One of China's most sought-after contemporary artists, He Qi (pronounced huh chee) is a professor of art at Nanjing Union Theological Seminary. As a child he was taught to paint by his father's friend, the former chair of the art department of Nanjing University. Later, as teenager during the Cultural Revolution, He Qi was sent with his family to do hard field labor after his father's university was closed down. Here He Qi began to paint portraits of Mao and was eventually relieved from his field work by winning a painting competition. Subsequently, having been exposed to the great Renaissance artists by his Paris-trained teacher, he began to learn from the masters of Western art and of the Middle Ages. He speaks of painting Mao by day and Rafael's *Madonna* by night. But it was this painting by Rafael's which set his feet on the Christian path. Immersed in a climate of political unrest and social struggles, he found himself deeply moved by the peace he saw in the Madonna's eyes. It is this peace that the message of the Gospels proclaims that prevails in all of He Qi's art.

After the Cultural Revolution subsided, He Qi studied medieval art in Germany, later living in the United States. Still continuing to produce and teach art, he has had exhibitions in many countries around the world. His works express the brilliance, color and vitality of the Christian faith. Whereas Chinese Zen art is expressed in black with little or no color, He Qi seeks to communicate in his art the life-giving creativity of God. His bright color-on-paper paintings combine traditional Chinese painting techniques with those of Western art.

the bearer of the promised Messiah, whose reign will have no end. Mary's response was a joyous outburst of the words we have come to call the Magnificat—a song that glorifies and praises God for choosing her to be the blessed mother of Jesus. Luke then tells us that Mary stayed on with Elizabeth for about three months before returning to her own home.

THE PAINTING—LOOKING

In He Qi's painting the scene takes place outside on a cobblestoned street of a Chinese village. Two women stand in close contact with each other in stillness and gentleness. They hold hands in a moment of intimacy and deep, hushed peace and acceptance. Perhaps this moment in the painting comes after Elizabeth has exclaimed: "Blessed among women are you, and blessed is the fruit of your womb."

On the left side of the painting Mary, the more youthful of the two women, stands with her head bowed and covered with a veil. Her eyes are closed, a suggestion that she has begun to ponder these things in her heart (Luke 2:19). Hers is a posture of humility and receptivity. At the time of the angel's visit she may have questioned this amazing act of God in her life. By the end of the angel's announcement, she expressed her acceptance of her calling with the words, "Be it done to me according to your word." Her right arm, folded protectively across her stomach, indicates the precious gift that she holds within. As she stands with Elizabeth, we see her completely, humbly and peacefully surrendered to God's will.

Elizabeth stands on the right of the painting. Her body suggests a more mature woman, one who is further along in her own pregnancy than Mary. Her eyes are wide open. Could this be suggestive of her transformed vision, her spiritual insights, or her recognition of the movement of the Spirit of God? She holds Mary's hand in support and encouragement. In her other hand she carries a water pitcher.

The two figures are completely alone in their encounter. There are no witnesses to their conversation, but we sense that this is a holy moment. They stand in sacred space highlighted by the pure brilliance of the white walls behind them.

COMPANIONS ON THE WAY

The artist has placed the women in the middle of an empty street. This serves as a visual reminder that as travelers on the Way, we are all in need of soul hospitality that offers safety, generous space and silence in which to share our journey. Elizabeth seems to have been on an errand, perhaps to the well for water. But she stops to listen to Mary, her empty pitcher in her hand. For her, the rest of the world stands still and her entire focus is on Mary. Her eyes are fixed on Mary, her body turned toward her and her attention uninterrupted by anything else around her.

Notice that the two women meet on the street. Mary has hurried over to Elizabeth to announce her news. In this painting they meet each other not in Elizabeth's home but en route to her house. The initial excitement of their meeting has been replaced by silence and attentiveness. Mary is welcomed right where she is with a response that is immediate and warmly inviting. Acutely aware of Mary's pressing need to share her story, Elizabeth attends to her without hesitation.

Elizabeth is not reluctant to touch and be touched by Mary. She reaches out and holds Mary's hand in a gesture of acceptance and encouraging support. Even though she herself has been wondrously favored by God with a child in her old age, she is keenly alert and responsive to Mary's own story. She has laid aside her own concerns, her own story, in order to give undivided attention to Mary. In doing so, she clears a wide-open space where the two of them may listen to the leading of the Spirit.

By opening her heart and home to Mary, Elizabeth has offered her space and safety—soul hospitality where Mary can share her journey without reservations or fear. This is a relationship of trust and openness. Having heard Mary's story of the miraculous visitation by the angel Gabriel, Elizabeth's child within her leaped, and Elizabeth was filled with the Spirit. For Elizabeth this was an affirmation of the work of the Spirit of God not only in her own life but more importantly in Mary's. Together both women must have sensed this very real and close presence of God.

As we look further at the painting, we sense an atmosphere of stillness and silence as Mary and Elizabeth meet. In order to really listen to Mary, Elizabeth is depicted with one hand at her side, her mouth closed and her eyes wide open. She says nothing, listens without distraction and notices much. She appears to be listening with her whole being as she bends her head toward Mary with her body directed completely toward her.

Elizabeth has laid aside her own concerns, her emptying of self and her own preoccupations. We see this symbolically portrayed in the empty pitcher she holds in her left hand. For this moment in time she has forgotten about her errand to the village well in order to give her full attention to another. The emptiness of the container highlights her openness as well as the confidentiality of this awesome event that has been shared with her. In a sense Elizabeth is a container for Mary's story, receiving it and holding it with reverence as a sacred gift. Remember that this is sacred space where God is present.

It is possible to push the symbolism even further by suggesting that the water container represents the presence of the Holy Spirit in this relationship. The Spirit, often metaphorically associated with water or rain in the Bible, may be seen as present in this encounter. God has met both women, has blessed and miraculously gifted each one, and now they wait together in stillness to receive the Spirit's direction.

With her eyes open to the mystery of the Spirit, Elizabeth is given spiritual insight into Mary's experience of God. Here in the painting she seems to look beyond Mary to somewhere deeper and farther away—to unseen spiritual realities. Her verbal expression as well as the leaping of the child within her confirms that what she has heard is indeed from God, and that this event in Mary's life is a fulfillment of God's word.

Having shared her story, Mary then stayed on at Elizabeth's house, receiving continued support, encouragement, protection and space. Mary was not left to struggle with any lingering doubts or fears on her own. Instead, she was given ongoing spiritual nurture in an atmosphere of safety and warm hospitality for the next three months. Within a relationship of trust and with the guidance of the Spirit, both women must have discerned together when the time was right for Mary to return to her own home.

Notice that both women in this depiction are about the same height. There seems to be some mutuality here. Both appear open and vulnerable, seemingly waiting for something. Both stand in humble obedience as they listen for and attend to the movement of the Spirit. Elizabeth does not present herself as an authority but rather as one who humbly unites herself with another, sharing in Mary's journey.

JOURNEYING TOGETHER—RESPONDING

Since we all travel on the same journey toward God, we are all called in one way or another to share in each other's story. Like Mary, we are also invited to incarnate God in our lives, living out God's life in the midst of every life experience. When we accompany others, offering them soul hospitality and space to share their experience of God, we become more aware of the sacred in others. We become more ready and available to accompany them in discerning this presence, celebrating the glorious work of God as we watch with awe and gratitude the transformation—the new birth—that God is continually doing to transform us.

The prophet Isaiah's invitation is extended to us to be attentive to this new life being birthed in us.

Behold, I will do something new,
Now it will spring forth;
Will you not be aware of it? (Isaiah 43:19)

This is an invitation to be more aware, more fully open to the movement of the Spirit of God within yourself and in others. As you continue on your spiritual journey, be attentive to how the life of the Spirit is transforming you and those who share this Way with you. Recognize the holy in others and in yourself, and like both Mary and Elizabeth, praise God for the ongoing, transforming work of the Spirit.

FOR REFLECTION AND DISCUSSION

- Return to the text and reflect again on He Qi's painting. Who has accompanied you on your journey to help you become aware of the new life of Christ that is being birthed within you? Who are the people in your life who have been present to you to share in your celebration of this life? Who are the wisdom figures in your life who have brought fresh vision and insight into your experiences of God?

- Consider the ways you may have been such a person to another. How have you provided soul hospitality for someone else? How attentive are you to the movements of the Spirit in others? Where have you offered holy stillness and silence, sacred space, for someone to share their story?

- Be a participant in this miraculous encounter. How has this painting opened your eyes to new ways of responding to God and others?

- Mary may be called the first Christian, because she was the first to receive the living Lord into her being. Like Mary we are also called to be bearers of Christ. When we receive his life and choose to follow him, we bear his image to the world. How aware are you of this fact? What does this image look like?

12

BEARING CHRIST

RUBENS

The Descent from the Cross

*C*entral to Christian spirituality is the act of surrendering our will and all of our life to God. We do so not in response to power or out of fear, but in response to God's love. God's very character is love—a love that is extravagant and reckless, risking everything to draw us into intimacy. God desires a close relationship with us and always is the initiator of this love, reaching out to us even when we are most unlovable. Jesus calls us to join in the same intimate relationship that he shares with his Father. It is an invitation of friendship and of partnership with God. Even more, it is being united with him together with the Father and the Spirit in such depth and closeness that we are drawn into his very life. This new life direction involves a turning from our own self-oriented way of life to a life that is focused on God—on finding God's way and following in that way.

The disciples of Jesus were totally committed to Jesus from the very beginning of their call. They followed even when there were risks to their own lives. They may not have completely understood all of the implications of the life and death of Jesus, but they entrusted their lives to him and went with him. Their discipleship was costly, but their commitment remained strong in the face of trials and opposition. At Jesus' death, Joseph of Arimathea dared to go to Pilate to ask permission to take his body from the cross in order to bury it. He refused to be daunted by the dangers this would have involved for him.

DESCENT FROM THE CROSS—LISTENING

We find this story in John 19:38-42. Give it a long, slow reading. You may also like to read the accounts of the other Gospels (Matthew 27:57-61; Mark 15:42-47; Luke 23:50-56). If you do, notice the individual details each writer includes in his reporting of this poignant moment. Allow yourself to be present with Joseph and the other disciples who gathered together to remove the body of Jesus. What is your experience of being there? Imagine talking with the participants, and notice your own responses.

> After these things Joseph of Arimathea, being a disciple of Jesus, but a secret one for fear of the Jews, asked Pilate that he might take away the body of Jesus; and Pilate granted permission. So he came and took away His body.
>
> Nicodemus, who had first come to Him by night, also came, bringing a mixture of myrrh and aloes, about a hundred pounds weight.
>
> So they took the body of Jesus and bound it in linen wrappings with the spices, as is the burial custom of the Jews.
>
> Now in the place where He was crucified there was a garden, and in the garden a new tomb in which no one had yet been laid.
>
> Therefore because of the Jewish day of preparation, since the tomb was nearby, they laid Jesus there.

Now turn to Rubens's painting on this theme, *Descent from the Cross.** All four Gospels tell us that Joseph of Arimathea took Jesus' body down, wrapped it in a linen cloth and laid it in a tomb. Rubens chooses this dramatic moment of the descent of Jesus' body into the waiting arms of his devoted followers for his artistic meditation. His painting depicts the interaction of people who were already surrendered to God's love. Let us see what this surrender looks like. Take your time for a careful look at the painting. Be open to whatever gifts God has for you through this experience.

What is your initial response to this painting? What is the first thing you see? How does this work support your reading of the biblical story? Let's look together at how Rubens expresses his own meditation on canvas. But first it is important for us to consider some of the historical context and the artist's intent behind this painting.

The legend of St. Christopher. Painted to encourage and inspire the faithful, *The Descent from the Cross* is the central panel of a triptych that Rubens painted for the Cathedral of Our Lady in Antwerp, Belgium. The left panel of the altarpiece depicts Mary's visit to Elizabeth, and the right, the presentation of the baby Jesus in the temple. It was commissioned by a group whose patron saint was St. Christopher, the patron saint of travelers. Very briefly, as legend has it, St. Christopher was on a quest to find and serve the most powerful ruler in the world. After many adventures without success, he was asked by a small child to be carried across a river. When he took the child on his shoulders, he found him to be unbearably heavy. He later discovered that the child was none other than Christ, who was so heavy because he bore the sinful weight of the whole world. From then on, having found the mightiest sovereign of the world, the saint gave his life over to Christ and served him until his martyrdom.

---

*On the Internet go to <www.abcgallery.com/R/rubens/rubens112.html>.

Peter Paul Rubens (1577-1640)

Considered to be the most popular Flemish artist of the seventeenth century, Peter Paul Rubens was born in Germany. His Protestant father, a lawyer, had fled with his family from Antwerp because of persecution for his Calvinist faith. After his death the family moved back to Antwerp, where Rubens converted to the Catholic faith. There he was well-educated in the classics and several languages. He pursued further art education in Italy for eight years, where he was greatly influenced by Michelangelo and the Venetian artists. He returned to Antwerp after his mother's death and was rebaptized as a Catholic.

Rubens was well-trained not only in painting but in printmaking, drawing, book illustrating, tapestry design, sculpture and architecture as well. Noted for his exuberant baroque style, which emphasized movement, color and sensuality, Rubens had a large workshop with many apprentices

In response to the Reformation, Rubens created art for the church with the intent to speak directly to the senses and the emotions rather than through reason. He had an encyclopedic knowledge of religious symbolism and classical mythology, which he used to great effect in his biblical art. His religious paintings reflect the dynamic movement, monumentality and exaggerated naturalism of baroque art. *The Descent from the Cross* was painted in 1612-1614.

Regardless of the historicity of this legend, it does hold the key to the meaning of Rubens's altarpiece. St. Christopher's name literally means Christ-bearer. All the men and women in the panels, especially the central panel, are Christ-bearers. Let's look together at its implications for us.

THE PAINTING—LOOKING

Rubens's painting shows Jesus being lowered from the cross by his grieving friends. Placed in the center of the scene, he is the focal point of the painting. Our eyes are immediately drawn to the sweeping diagonal line made by the shining white shroud against which the limp, lifeless body of Jesus rests. This linen cloth will be used to wrap the naked body of Jesus (remember that the soldiers had cast lots for his clothing). This strong line accentuates Jesus' complete abandonment in death. It epitomizes the original descent from the light of heaven to a dark world in need of redemption.

Notice how the blood drips from his head, hands and side, staining the white cloth and flowing down to those below. It describes Christ's utter obedience to his Father to the point of offering himself as a sacrifice on a cruel cross. The face of Christ reflects a life that has been selflessly surrendered, poured out for the whole world. His head dangles to one side and his body hangs lifelessly in death and vulnerably exposed. The skin of his body—arms, legs and lips—bears the greenish-yellow pallor of death. Rubens's intent was to evoke an emotional response from the viewer—this Christ is indeed dead. And his death was for all. What is your initial response? Are you moved, revolted or drawn into the story? An immediate response to this painting at retreats and seminars I have led is stunned silence and awe. Today we talk about Jesus' death on the cross without really thinking about its starkly brutal reality. This painting makes it tangibly realistic, and it moves me also to silence and tears. It brings home to me the enormous and awesome sacrifice that Jesus made for humankind in his death on the cross.

In the background the billows of black clouds still linger from the dark hours of the crucifixion. They remind us of the dramatic events that accompanied this death—earthquakes and darkness, and a rending of the veil in the temple. A further reference to the horrific death can be seen when we look closely at the bottom right corner of the painting. Lying at the foot of the ladder is the paper with the inscription—INRI, Jesus Christ King of the Jews—and a rock which may refer to Jesus as the rock of our salvation. We may perhaps think of the rock as the instrument used to nail the inscription to the cross. Next to these lies a platter that holds the crown of thorns and some of the blood that has dripped from the thorns. The dish resembles the paten on which the Communion bread was placed before it was given to the believers. In this way the artist connects it to the eucharistic celebration of the bread and wine. Salvation has been secured because of this sacrificial offering, which would bring light and freedom to those who believe. A hint of this is symbolically included in the artist's interpretation. Look at the sky on the left side of the painting, behind the figure of Mary, the mother of Jesus. It is beginning to lighten as the inky clouds slowly dissipate. Perhaps this is also a reference to the resurrection to come and to which this group will be witnesses.

A CLOSER LOOK

But who are the participants in Rubens's painting? Clustered around Jesus like bunches of grapes on the vine, Jesus' close friends carefully cooperate in lowering his body from the cross. The sap that flows from this vine is love, which unites them in this moment of surrender. It is to this love that they have surrendered, and it means life to these lovers of Jesus. Perhaps they remembered Jesus' words that he is the vine and they are the branches, drawing their very sustenance from him. All display their love and devotion to Jesus in eyes and gestures that touch our own hearts and move us to respond.

Let us look at these disciples and try to identify them. Starting at the left corner, we see the three Marys mentioned as being present in the other accounts—Mary, the mother of Jesus; Mary Magdalene; and Mary, the mother of Joses. We are given clues to their identity through their clothing and postures. Mary, Jesus' mother, whose blue gown traditionally identifies her in art, reaches

achingly upward to her son. Her grieving face is lit by the whiteness of the cloth and reflects her broken-hearted sorrow. Her skin
matches the ashen pastiness of Jesus', and we remember Simeon's
prophesy at the presentation in the temple that a sword would
pierce her heart. She seems as vulnerable as her son in this depiction, and we can barely imagine her profound sense of loss.

The other two women kneel at the feet of Jesus. One supports
his foot as it rests on her shoulder. This is an important clue to her
identity. It was Mary Magdalene who washed Jesus' feet with her
tears and dried them with her hair. Here we see her hair lying
loosely around her shoulders as she tenderly caresses and supports
his foot with her hands. The other Mary looks up toward Jesus
with almost an incredulous expression while she holds the end of
the sheet. With Magdalene she declares on her expectant features
her faith and hope that the promise of Jesus' coming to life again
would be realized. The women cannot offer help to the men in re-
leasing the body of Jesus, but their contribution is just as valuable
and important. They await its final descent, when they can anoint
it for burial with the spices they have brought. Their presence em-
phasizes the pathos of the scene.

Now move your eyes up from Jesus' mother. Standing on a ladder
above Mary is a person who figures prominently in the story. It is
Joseph of Arimathea. We know this because he is the one who is the
most sumptuously dressed among the men. He is described in Matthew's Gospel as a wealthy man. He was able to afford a new tomb,
which he had purchased for his own eventual burial. Jesus will be
buried in this tomb. The light that radiates from the cloth that he
holds reflects on his face. He does not look at Jesus but seems to be
looking across at a figure in black or dark blue. What is it that connects these two people, and who is this shadowy follower?

We are told in John that Nicodemus came also with Joseph to
take down Jesus' body. Remember how Nicodemus came to be a
disciple of Jesus. He was a Pharisee who went to Jesus under cover

of darkness because he was afraid of being discovered (John 3:1-2). Rubens paints him in dark clothing, appropriate for covert rendezvous. His body twists almost painfully as he clumsily does his part. He seems also to be looking at Joseph as together they share a collusive discipleship for fear of the Jews. Their eyes connect them to each other and indicate to us their identities.

The person down from Nicodemus is a commanding presence in red. He seems to bear the full weight of the body as it makes its descent. He is John who has been described as the beloved disciple and who is identifiable in art by his red clothing. Here he leans backward under his burden, awkwardly resting his right foot on the rung of the ladder on which Nicodemus is perched. Follow with your eyes the line of blood that flows from Jesus' left hand, down the sheet, toward the wounded side and the loincloth. Continue downward and it seems to form a large pool in the man's red clothing. Look even further down and we see that the blood has ended its descent in the dish that holds the crown of thorns. The life of Jesus is being poured into John—almost as if he is receiving a transfusion. Jesus' shed blood gives new life and meaning to those who surrender themselves to his love. It creates a new level of intimacy between humans and God.

John holds Jesus' legs and side, yet he too seems to be focused somewhere else. Look at where his eyes are focused. He gazes at Mary, Jesus' mother. We remember the words of Jesus from the cross to John and to his mother: "Woman, behold, your son. . . . Behold, your mother" (John 19:26-27). John is depicted here as already showing care and concern for Mary in her sorrow. In fact, right after the crucifixion John had taken her into his own home to care for her as his own mother.

At the top of the painting, two rough-looking men hang precariously from the crossbeams. One is clothed simply and holds the cloth in his mouth as he takes particular care to prevent the body from falling. The upper body of the other is bare and we see his strong muscles rippling with tension as his right hand gently releases Jesus to those below him. He hangs on the beam of the cross with his leg so perilously extended out behind him that we are tempted to shout to him to be careful. We don't know for sure who these two are, but we can safely assume that they are two of the former fishermen who followed Jesus. Could the man on the right be Peter? We often associate him with impetuous behavior, and here he grasps the cloth with his teeth—using any help he can to be gentle with his beloved Lord.

ONE BODY—RESPONDING

All the attendants in this stirring scene handle Jesus with tenderness and gentleness. Notice that each one is physically touching Jesus or is just removing their hand as the weight of his body shifts from one person to the next. They are each closely linked to him physically and emotionally. Each provides, in their own way, care and dignity to one who has suffered the most ignoble of deaths. They are united in their grief and in their attention. They are focused on their task, but Rubens's depiction through their glances suggests a care for each other as well. The corporate community of the faithful forms itself into a single body around the body of Christ. It is this central theme of Christ's crucifixion for all people that establishes the foundation for his church. Each participant has become a Christ-bearer imitating Christ in self-sacrificial service and love. Each one present at this scene has taken the risk of being exposed and persecuted.

In this vivid visual rendition we see that this is indeed "My body, which is for you," the one that we receive at Communion (1 Corinthians 11:24). Consider for a moment where this painting was intended to be placed—above the altar of the cathedral. Below this altarpiece, the Eucharist or Communion was administered. If we were to continue the line of descent and allow the body to fall to its ultimate resting place, we may be surprised to discover that

Jesus' body eventually ends up on the Communion Table. How much more realistic could this sacrifice have been for the faithful in Rubens's time?

The Christians who went forward to partake of this food would not have missed its powerful impact and significance. This same body depicted above is still being received by Jesus' followers in the sacramental form of broken bread. The figures in the painting receive the actual body as something precious and sacred. So too do the worshipers who take to themselves this holy sacrament. The mystery of this profound reenactment makes its participants Christ-bearers along with those who were present for Jesus at his deposition. They all receive eternal life and are brought into fellowship with the Father through this death.

FOR REFLECTION AND DISCUSSION

- Reread the story of this event in John and then return to the painting. What has changed for you as you review the scene? What new observations do you notice?

- Step into the painting and notice where you would stand or kneel. How does it feel to participate with the disciples of Jesus? What is your contribution as you cooperate with them? With whom do you feel connected, and what draws you to that person?

- We cannot actually handle the body of Jesus as these people did, but when we take the bread and wine of the Eucharist into our hands we are entering into this very act through the mystery of the sacrament. What effect does this meditation have on you when you receive this sacrament? How aware are you of being a Christ-bearer? How completely does Jesus' blood fill and transform you?

- In surrendering to God's love our lives are no longer ordinary. We take on the mind, heart and life of God and become Christ to the world. How is your life being transformed into the extraordinary life of Christ as you take in the bread and wine of this sacred act?

SEEING AND SERVING

LUCA GIORDANO
The Good Samaritan

∞

*T*he life of Jesus was a life of love, which means that Jesus spent his life on earth reaching out to everyone, especially to those who were considered outcasts and undesirables. Recall the number of times he was criticized for associating with sinners, touching lepers and dead bodies, and flaunting the established conventions of his day by giving dignity and worth to women. He saw value and worth in each person who came to him. There was no one who was excluded from his loving gaze and welcoming embrace.

Jesus constantly invited his followers to change their way of seeing others. Bringing together a community of disparate individuals he provided a pattern for them to love each other and live in unity and humility. They were encouraged to be as inclusive as he was in the way they related to those outside of their circle. The love and care they showed to him at his death and burial was to be extended to the world—even to those who were not considered deserving or acceptable. This company of Christ-followers was called to see with his eyes of love and to respond with his heart of compassion.

Centuries later we are still being invited to change our perspective—to move beyond ourselves to reach out with compassion and love to those who are least like us. It takes not only renewed vision but a transformed life to be able to follow Christ's way of self-denial and self-sacrifice. Jesus used parables to illustrate much of what he taught and to challenge his listeners to examine themselves more closely, prompting them to shift their assumptions and core belief systems. Parables shock us into awareness, teaching us how to be transformed from the inside out. Instead of confirming our own small ways of being, they uproot our established ideas of how things should be, moving us beyond ourselves. The familiar story of the good Samaritan comes immediately to mind when we consider this radical way of living.

THE PARABLE—LISTENING

Get comfortable in a quiet place and turn to the story in Luke 10:30-37. Read it very slowly and contemplatively as if for the first time, allowing it to absorb your full attention. Accompany the men on their journey as you read, and notice any details that may surface for you. What was your experience like? How were you more aware of what was happening in the story?

> Jesus replied and said, "A man was going down from Jerusalem to Jericho, and fell among robbers, and they stripped him and beat him, and went away leaving him half dead.
>
> "And by chance a priest was going down on that road, and when he saw him, he passed by on the other side.
>
> "Likewise a Levite also, when he came to the place and saw him, passed by on the other side.
>
> "But a Samaritan, who was on a journey, came upon him; and when he saw him, he felt compassion,
>
> and came to him and bandaged up his wounds, pouring oil

and wine on them; and he put him on his own beast, and brought him to an inn and took care of him.

"On the next day he took out two denarii and gave them to the innkeeper and said, 'Take care of him; and whatever more you spend, when I return I will repay you.'

"Which of these three do you think proved to be a neighbor to the man who fell into the robbers' hands?"

And he said, "The one who showed mercy toward him." Then Jesus said to him, "Go and do the same."

Before we look at the painting by Giordano, let's consider the context of this parable. In the preceding verses we read that a young lawyer had come to Jesus to put him to the test by asking how he could inherit eternal life. Jesus' response was to sum up the whole law in the following: "You shall love the Lord your God with all your heart, and with all your soul, and with all your strength, and with all your mind; and your neighbour as yourself." The lawyer's further question as to who was his neighbor prompted Jesus to reply with a shocking parable.

A Jewish man on his way from Jerusalem to Jericho was attacked and robbed by thieves. It was a road notoriously known for this kind of dangerous assault. He was beaten badly, stripped of everything he owned and then left on the road half-dead. Two religious men, one a priest and the other a Levite, passed him and crossed to the other side, perhaps to avoid becoming ceremoniously unclean, failing to offer him any help. A third man, a Samaritan, saw the unfortunate traveler, felt compassion for him and came to his aid. Jesus knew well the commonly held opinion of Samaritans in his day. They were considered to be on the same level as Gentiles and treated as such—bitterly despised, socially and religiously shunned, and treated with animosity and hostility.

When we read this story today we can easily miss the shock the story would have been greeted with. For a Samaritan to be the protagonist, the one to offer mercy and help to a Jew, was outrageous and scandalous. Yet Jesus uses him to make his point. His listeners would have been astounded at this example of who their neighbor should be. The priest and the Levite, righteous and upright members of society, should have been the ones to be held up as examples to emulate. But they were the ones in the parable who walked by and who made a conscious effort to steer clear of the wounded man. Jesus was encouraging a radically different perspective by having a Samaritan extend compassion and help to a Jew—utterly contrary to expectations. He shattered traditional definitions of who was an outcast and who was righteous.

THE PAINTING—LOOKING

Take a long, slow look at Giordano's painting *The Good Samaritan.*[*] A figure stoops down to pour oil and wine on a dying man's wounds. They occupy a rocky landscape that is dark and forbidding. In the distance the light shines on the town both men were headed to. How is this different from the image you may have created in your imagination? What are you drawn to in this depiction? What emotions or associations surfaced for you?

Let's look first at the Samaritan who offers help to the poor traveler. Himself a traveler on this dark, dangerous and rocky road, he pauses on his journey to attend to the man's needs. His horse patiently stands behind him, looking calmly at his master's efforts. Oblivious to everything around him, the Samaritan's gaze is fully focused on his task. His face seems to suggest anger at the atrocious brutality that has been inflicted. His brow is furrowed with concern and worry for this dying man.

He holds a container in his right hand. It contains the oil or wine mentioned in the story. He uses this to moisten the cloth in

---

[*]On the Internet go to <www.1st-art-gallery.com/thumbnail/89549/1/The-Good-Samaritan-1685.jpg>.

Luca Giordano (1634-1705)

Born in Naples, Italy, Giordano was a prolific decorative artist. Steeped in the culture and religion of his day, his themes were primarily religious and mythological. His father was a mediocre painter who saw opportunity for financial gain from his son's talents at an early age. He urged Luca to produce works as fast as he could with the words "Luca fa presto," which earned Luca the nickname "Luke Work-Fast." He obeyed his father so completely that he rarely stopped work to eat. Fed by his father as he painted, he produced a vast body of works because of his speed and versatility.

Giordano studied in Rome and traveled extensively, absorbing many influences, especially those of Raphael and Michelangelo, whose paintings he copied with great skill. Later as court painter to Charles II of Spain, he spent ten years producing commissions of frescoes for churches, ceilings and palaces before returning to Naples where he lived until his death.

The Good Samaritan, painted in 1685, hangs in the Musée de Beaux-Arts, Rouen, France.

his left hand to cleanse the man's open and bleeding wounds. He does this with such care and gentleness that we know his concern is genuine, even though this is a complete stranger. Look at the tender way his hand presses on the open wound. His stooped posture suggests the humility and self-forgetting that Jesus expressed in his incarnation. Extending compassion on a lonely road, the Samaritan does not care that he is absorbing the dust and perhaps the blood of the man. Nor does he seem to care that the attackers could still be in hiding close by and about to pounce on him too. He exposes himself to the danger and risk of losing his own life.

The horse in the painting alludes to what will take place after this initial attention. The parable tells us that the Samaritan's kindness stretched even further. He not only washed and dressed his wounds, but put him on his own animal and took him to an inn to recuperate. There he took care of him for the night before moving on, but not before paying for his stay and offering to repay the innkeeper for any further costs that could arise in his absence. This is utter self-sacrifice, which costs him time, money, clothes, wine and oil. The word *compassion* literally means "to suffer with." It has been described by Mary Jo Meadow as a "quivering of the heart in response to another's suffering." It means living out our faith in full awareness of and in response to everyone in our midst. We speak of walking in another person's shoes or getting inside another person's skin. In order to respond with genuine care for another, we must allow ourselves to be close enough to their suffering to feel it. We need to be connected with those who suffer, even when they are different from us or undeserving. This is the kind of compassion and mercy that we see here and that Jesus encourages. And this is the kind of attentiveness that the Samaritan offers to an "enemy."

Take a moment for a closer look at the wounded traveler. Notice the pallor of his skin, crisply defined and white against the dark and rugged rocks. His naked body lies in complete abandonment, his head lolling back lifelessly. Even though we cannot see his face, we sense his agony and distress by the way his hand is flung out beside him. It hangs as lifelessly as his head, with the fingers contorted in pain. He may be wincing from having his wound cleaned. If we doubt his closeness to death, we can verify his appalling condition from his posture and from his body drained of blood and color. The Samaritan is dressed in red and gold, and stands in vivid contrast to the whiteness of this body. The broken branch of a tree just above his head serves to emphasize the violence and ferocity of the attack. Could the thieves have been hiding in the tree and then fallen on the traveler from above, breaking the branch on their way down?

What associations come to you when you look at this body? Remember the previous painting by Rubens. The body in Giordano's painting bears a remarkable resemblance to Jesus'. The loincloth is similarly rendered, as is the sallowness of the skin. The wound in the man's chest is where the wound is on Jesus' body. The artist's rendering prompts us to consider Jesus' words in Matthew 25:40: "To the extent that you did it to one of these brothers of Mine, even the least of them, you did it to Me." It is an awesome mystery that when we extend mercy and love to our neighbor, we are actually ministering to Jesus himself.

THE EYES OF GOD,
THE HEART OF GOD—RESPONDING

Jesus presses home his point in this parable—those who are least deserving, those who are marginalized and least like us, are ones to whom we must show compassion. In his letter to the Philippians Paul exhorts us to put on the mind of Christ, to have the same attitude Jesus had. He reminds us of Jesus' self-emptying in giving up his heavenly prerogatives when he descended in abandonment and healing love. There is a Jewish proverb that says that most people will not see God because they will not stoop low enough. We are called to stoop as low as Jesus did, to imitate him, in order to touch others with his love. This is a love that turns the world upside down. It is a transformed awareness which in turn transforms our world where we begin to see our neighbor as equally precious to and loved by God as we are. When we look at the outsiders and the unlovely in our midst, we can see God in them because the eyes of our heart have been transformed.

The heart of God is a heart of compassion. God sees our pain and suffering, and enters into our experience to bring us freedom and healing. It is easier for us to bear others if we remember that

Christ carries us, bearing the entire weight on his shoulders. It helps us to envision Christ carrying not only myself but also those whom I carry. When our eyes and heart are aligned with those of God, our living is transformed and we become more and more like Christ. In response to the question of how she could love and minister to the poorest of the poor in India, Mother Teresa is reported to have said that she was able to do the lowly work of caring for the poor and destitute of Calcutta because she saw the face of Christ in each one who came for help. Because God's love has been shown to us, we are called to reach out to others with that same love— God in us responding to God in the other.

Writing in the fourteenth century, Teresa of Ávila expressed how we become Christ to others when we reach out in love to them. Spend a moment reflecting on the truths she reminds us of.

> Christ has no body now but yours,
> No hands, no feet on earth but yours,
> Yours are the eyes with which he looks
> With compassion on this world,
> Yours are the feet with which he walks to do good,
> Yours are the hands, with which he blesses all the world,
> Yours are the hands, yours are the feet.
> Yours are the eyes, you are his body.
> Christ has no body now but yours,
> No hands, no feet on earth but yours,
> Yours are the eyes with which he looks
> With compassion on this world.
> Christ has no body now on earth but yours.

Jesus' question to the lawyer is also addressed to us. Who is your neighbor? How do you show mercy and love to those who are outside of your company? Reaching out to others is costly, and we may be inclined to feel that we don't have enough for ourselves to share. It is good to remember the account of Jesus feeding the five thousand. When confronted with the people's need for food Jesus asked his disciples how much bread they had. He told them to go and look. He subtly reminded them that the bread was already there. All they needed were eyes to see the available resources. If we offer our own limited resources to God, seeking to share them out of generosity and love, God takes them, blesses them, multiplies them and uses them to nurture and help others. In the Gospel account the people were not only fed but satisfied. Working hand in hand with God as we live compassionately in the world, we are copartners in strengthening and growing the kingdom of God on earth. Open eyes result in open hearts and hands.

FOR REFLECTION AND DISCUSSION

- Return to the parable with renewed eyes and allow it to mirror back to you your own inner attitudes. How has your perception of the story changed after looking at the painting? What has shifted in your heart after your meditation on both the text and the painting? What invitations did you receive?

- Place yourself in the painting and live as both characters. Take a moment to be the Samaritan and then to be the beaten man. What part does each play in your spiritual life?

- Now imaginatively live as the priest and the Levite, who are not included in the artist's depiction. What does it feel like to turn away from someone in need? Who is your neighbor in today's world? Who do you consider to be righteous and unrighteous in society?

- Remember the Jewish proverb? Most people will not see God because they will not stoop low enough. Some people cannot see what is in front of them; others just choose not to. The priest and the Levite walked by, refusing to even look at the man. How and when have you avoided looking at someone in need and walked past them without offering mercy? What keeps you from stooping down to the level of the oppressed and needy?

- If we believe Jesus' words that caring for the needy is somehow the same as attending to him, how do you view the people in your world who are considered pariahs to be shunned? How do you love your neighbor as your very own being?

- In sacrificing ourselves for others we lose our life only to find it again. Jesus shows us how to do this perfectly in extravagantly throwing away his life to give us an unimaginably richer life. He did not cling to anything but squandered himself even to death. How do we mirror his life as we try to live with fearless generosity and abandoned love? How is Christ increasing in you? How are you decreasing?

EPILOGUE

TRANSFORMING VISION

ೕ

No one would ever deny the importance of being able to see with our physical eyes. To be without sight or to be visually impaired implies a life that is enormously limited in all aspects. Being spiritually blind has the same confining effect, narrowing how we see, live and relate in the world. Spiritual sight is equally important to us because without it we would be limited in seeing God's action in our lives and therefore unable to respond. We are all familiar with the expression "blissfully unaware" in describing a way of being where we are almost unconscious, untroubled by circumstances around us. This may be fine for a short period of time, but to go through life in a state of mindless detachment disconnects us from God, ourselves and the world.

To be truly aware in this life is to be truly alive—something that God deeply desires for each one of us because it brings glory to God. Being awake to God's presence in all of life means that we see God in everything, not just in the good times but in the painful and desperate struggles of life. When we live in this consciously awake state, God becomes centrally important to and a full participant in whatever may come into our lives. It is this kind of awareness, of seeing God in all things, which gradually makes a difference in the core of our being—in our very heart.

When Jesus invites us to follow him, he is inviting us to a changed perspective, which in turn gradually makes our hearts of stone into hearts of flesh. His love brings transformation to our hearts and restores us as children of God. Instead of hard and impenetrable hearts, Jesus desires molten hearts on which God may write his letter of love. Paul reminds us that we are a letter of Christ and that this letter is written "not with ink but with the Spirit of the living God, not on tablets of stone, but on tablets of human hearts" (2 Corinthians 3:3). We are a letter for all to read—a letter which either proclaims the glory of the living God or promotes the kingdom of self.

A new vision embraces how we see, a transformed heart and a changed way of living or responding to the world. How we see ourselves and the world will affect how we respond to them. When we learn how to see life through the eyes of God, we begin to see that God is in every moment and circumstance of our own lives. It is from this new perspective that we can align our heart with the heart of God and can then live out of a new center. This is what it means to take on the eyes, the mind and the heart of Christ.

We have been journeying prayerfully together through biblical passages and paintings, learning how to see. In looking at the paintings by Bruegel we may have come to recognize our own blindness, and may have responded to the invitations to have our vision restored. In response to these invitations we realize that we have to be intentional about how we see and about practicing awareness. It entails spending deliberate times of solitude and stillness with God, where we open ourselves in abandonment to whatever God wants to do in us. Jesus himself showed us in his wilderness retreat how to be fully present to God. We also saw this in Mary, who sat at Jesus' feet listening to his words, and in Millet's peasants, who stopped their busy work to be attentive to God in their midst.

Jesus invited the attention and worship of the shepherds at his birth. That invitation is still being offered to us to notice where he is—in our midst and initiating intimacy with us even when we are unaware of him. Like the disciples at Emmaus, on the boat in Galilee and in the upper room, we can also be surprised when we find Jesus to be present in all things. But we live more radically, with renewed and clearer vision, if we are alert to Jesus' presence wherever we are.

Life is never the same when we give everything to Jesus. Our life will be full of joy in the knowledge that we belong to the Father and that the Spirit of God lives in us. But suffering and struggle will always be a part of our humanity, and Jesus is the one who shows us how to bear the crosses in our lives. He walked with his cross to Golgotha, and calls us to follow him bearing our own cross. Surrendering to God's love we become bearers of Christ himself. We become Christ to others as we participate in their lives, helping them to see where God is present and working. As we reach out to the world we not only see with God's eyes but respond with his heart of love and compassion. Our transformed eyes, heart and life allows us to see others as God sees them. Then we are made free to reach out to everyone who needs mercy in just the way that Christ did to us.

What we have been doing throughout this book is prayer. As we have been engaging in these contemplative exercises we have been praying. Our eyes have been looking to our Lord, who gives us grace, mercy and love. Keeping our gaze focused on God, we join with the psalmist in expressing our dependence on God's grace:

> To You I lift up my eyes. . . .
> Our eyes look to the LORD our God,
> Until he is gracious to us. (Psalm 123:1-2)

May these meditations encourage you in your journey of faith to move forward with renewed awareness, new vision and transformed living in a life that will then *be* prayer.

APPENDIX 1

SUGGESTIONS FOR GROUP DISCUSSION LEADERS

◈

*T*his book lends itself not only to individual use but also to groups who will read a chapter and meet for group discussion and sharing. View this time not just as an opportunity to share ideas but as a time of contemplative prayer. Although ideally suited to smaller groups, I have found meditation on Christian art and Scripture to be powerful and transformational in larger gatherings too.

PREPARATION

In preparation for the group meeting, decide on how long you want to meet. While I have spent as long as a week leading a group through an extended meditation on a single painting, an hour and a half is generally adequate to discuss a chapter, share gifts and invitations received (and ways of responding to these), and spend some time in contemplative stillness before God, before the Word and before the related work of art. Remember, however, that this is a time of prayer and should never be rushed.

I would suggest that you encourage group participants to read the preface and chapter one before the first meeting. In this session you should begin by discussing the concepts and responses participants offer to the reflective questions I present in chapter one. Consider using about half of your first session for this. Then offer a lectio divina on the Scripture passage that forms the basis of the meditation in chapter two and spend the remainder of the session leading them through a meditation on the work of art that is presented in this chapter. (Lectio divina comes from the Latin and literally means divine reading or spiritual reading. It is a way of engaging prayerfully with Scripture in order to hear God's personal word to you.) Encourage them to then read chapter two before the next session, when you will begin by discussing their insights from it and then lead them through a lectio of the passage and meditation on the art from chapter three. In this way, they will come to each without having generally read the chapter on the art you will discuss in that session. (See table 1 for a summary of this approach.)

Table 1. Outline of Sessions

Session	Participants Have Read	Share/Discuss	Lead Meditation on
1	Pref. and chap. 1	Pref. and chap. 1	Chap. 2
2	Chap. 2	Chap. 2	Chap. 3
3	Chap. 3	Chap. 3	Chap. 4
4	Chap. 4	Chap. 4	Chap. 5
Etc.			

Organized this way, each week you will introduce the passage and work of art that participants will read about and further meditate on during the time between group meetings.

In preparation for each session, you will, of course, need to take some quiet time to contemplatively read the next chapter and the related Scripture passage. Then do the same contemplative "reading" of the painting, drawing your own impressions from it and allowing it to engage all of your senses. Follow this by slowly reading the meditation in the chapter and the reflective questions at the end. Allow the meditation to first speak to you before you seek to help others articulate how it has spoken to them.

Create a contemplative, quiet space that supports contemplative silence and stillness for your group. Retreat centers naturally provide such a space with plenty of room for quiet reflection in chapels, gardens or secluded niches. But any place that is conducive to reflection and solitude encourages prayer. Many places can be creatively prepared to support contemplative prayer.

You may want to define your space by having a lit candle (symbolic of the Holy Spirit's presence) or placing some other physical cues to remind you to be attentive to God's presence. You might choose to set up a simple visual center—such as draped fabric with vials of oil and wine for the story of the good Samaritan. Or, if you are praying the story of Christ's descent from the cross, you may use a long white sheet draped diagonally on a cross, with a dish below containing the crown of thorns, nails, sponge and so on. Use your imagination and creativity, but keep these cues as simple as possible. These physical reminders are merely helps to staying focused and attentive to God.

LEADING THE GROUP

Soft contemplative music as people enter the room helps to establish a sacred space. It also serves to invite stillness and prayerful silence. Once everyone is settled, light the candle and begin by offering a prayer of intention—a prayer that invites God to be present and prepares the group to be open to the Spirit's leading.

Introduce the chapter to be discussed, and in the first meeting explain how the time together will be used. Describe the process of reading Scripture contemplatively—as a way of listening rather than talking to God. Although there will be sharing and talking, there will be much time for silence and simply keeping company with God. Present the way you will be approaching the art as a prayer process, being attentive to God's presence, gifts and invitations that may arise.

Give a short explanation of the importance of seeing in the spiritual journey. Introduce the many ways that art has been important to the church and to faith through the ages. You may want to look together at Bruegel's *Census at Bethlehem* to help people become awake and more aware of how much they don't see what is right in front of their eyes.

Listening together. Read the biblical story a couple of times aloud with enough silence in between. Don't be afraid of silences—people are pondering what they have heard. Allow space for reflection on the text, then ask for a word or phrase that held their attention. Ask for the associations, memories or sensations that emerged out of this. Allow time for brief sharing of these.

Introduce the art and artist you will be considering, with reminders that the art is one artist's personal meditation on the biblical text. Some things may appear extraneous to the story, but exploring them together helps to open up new ways of seeing and responding to God.

Looking together. If your group is small enough, you may wish to provide each participant with a good reproduction of the painting. Better yet would be to project the image on a large screen so that everyone has a good view and can engage with it together. This means that the room you use should be able to be darkened to make all the details sharp and bright.

Allow people several minutes to look again at the painting, whether projected on a screen or on a page in their hands. When you feel they are ready, open up discussion by asking good, explicit questions: What do you see? What first catches your attention? What is your initial response to this painting? How does it make you feel? Responses should be short and direct at this point. It is amazing how varied and rich the experience of shared insights can be. We help each other to see more clearly with this kind of sharing.

Listen respectfully to each insight and observation, acknowledging them briefly. As their guide, walk through the painting with the group, paying attention to the details and their significance for spiritual transformation. Use the insights from the chapter in the book and also the reflective questions at the end of the chapter for further personal application. Perhaps the most important question to ask is where they might be in the painting. Ask them to insert themselves in the visual story and imagine where they would be and what they would be doing and experiencing. This is a way of further entering more fully into its time and meaning, drawing personal application and reference for their lives. And don't forget to leave lots of room for silence. Remember, this time together should be an experience of contemplative prayer, not simply discussion of ideas. Encourage sharing that expresses whatever invitations God may be offering. Give thanks to God for each gift as it is shared.

Responding personally. If there is time at the end, you may want to invite each participant to respond creatively to the meditation in their own way. This is a good time to let people go off by themselves to a quiet place for ten minutes or so to reflect further on the text and painting, and for them to journal about their experience, write a poem or explore whatever creative expression might be emerging in response to God's gifts.

Responding together. Gently bring the group back together at the end for a time of sharing the gifts and invitations they have received. Offer a closing prayer of gratitude for God's presence and for the transforming work of the Holy Spirit which has begun during this time.

APPENDIX 2

SUGGESTIONS FOR USE IN SPIRITUAL DIRECTION

*S*ince spiritual direction is the place where we are attentive to God's presence and action in a person's prayer life, offering contemplative space within the process is extremely important. The silence of contemplative space provides the ideal context for listening to the Holy Spirit, who is the true director. This is a stillness that makes room for the Spirit of God to be more readily recognized, received and responded to. It is this same silence and attentiveness that are engaged in the process of meditation on art.

When we approach a work of art contemplatively, we bring to it our focused attention, along with a readiness to be grasped by it. This opens us up to whatever gifts it may bring to our soul. In spiritual direction we share another person's experience of God in a space that allows surrender and response to God. This is why contemplation on art fits so well with the goals of spiritual direction. Even when a director has no interest in art or is not particularly "into art," there is great value in making it a part of the encounter. Be open to ways art may add to your time with those who you spiritually companion. As the Spirit leads you toward biblical passages that may draw the other person toward God or may shed light on their experience of God, you may want to find art that supports and encourages new ways of seeing.

PREPARATION

You may find it helpful in introducing the contemplative use of art in your spiritual direction to first share this book with your directee. If you do, suggest that they begin by reading the preface and first chapter as a way to understand the value of art as an aid to contemplative prayer, and discuss with them how this might fit with the work you are doing together in spiritual direction. If it appears that they are responsive to the use of art in your work together, consider encouraging that they work through the book and share with you their response to this. You might also, of course, encourage them to focus on particular works of art—either those discussed in the book or others you might be familiar with. Or, if you are aware of important spiritual issues they are struggling with and biblical passages that speak to this, you might use an Internet resource such as www.textweek.com to identify relevant works of art that you could then reproduce or use in your work together. To do this, follow the link to "Art Index" on the home page. It leads you to a page that organizes thousands of works of biblical art thematically, by book of the Bible and by lectionary reading.

LISTENING TOGETHER

If you do choose to work together on biblical art, consider beginning your session by listening together to the passage the art is based on. After a moment of silent prayer, read the text aloud slowly and prayerfully. Do this several times in a lectio divina format—leaving time for silence to attend to what they receive from the reading.

LOOKING TOGETHER

Then look together at a good reproduction of the piece of art. Explain how it will be used in a contemplative way—gazing in stillness and allowing it to broaden insight and deepen perception of spiritual realities. Allow your directee to take as long as he or she needs for a deep, slow and intense look at the painting. Start with basic questions such as What do you see? What do you sense or feel? What might God be saying to you? and How do you wish to respond? If you are working with one of the paintings from this book, you might also be able to use the reflective questions at the end of each chapter to enter more fully into the experience of the art and the text.

RESPONDING

As insights and responses are shared, take some time to hold them reverently before God in silence. Then thank God for the gifts received.

Encourage your directee to respond creatively to these gifts. Using creative expressions as a basis for contemplation evokes further creative expressions, and don't allow your directee to quickly dismiss the possibility that they could have within them sufficient creativity to respond in some uniquely personal way to the experience—journaling, creative writing, painting, drawing, photography, flower arranging or something as simple as cooking a meal that is a response to their engagement with the art and the Scripture behind it.

NOTES

Introduction

p. 12   the gaze of faith that is fixed on Jesus: Teresa of Ávila, cited in Anthony Delisi, *Praying in the Cellar: A Guide to Facing Your Fears and Finding God* (Orleans, Mass.: Paraclete Press, 2005), p. 141.

p. 12   "We live between the act of awakening": John O'Donohue, *Divine Beauty: The Invisible Embrace* (London: Transworld, 2003), p. 1.

p. 17   finding art on the Internet: All of the paintings referenced in this work can be located quite easily on the Internet by typing the name of the artist and painting in a search engine. Usually you will find many copies of the work of art; choose one that has high enough resolution to let you see it clearly. If you are searching by means of Google, you might also want to consider using Google Images rather than the Web; this will give you the actual art, rather than simply locations that may contain the art. Another option is to check some of the virtual art galleries that exist online. Some of the better galleries include the Web Gallery of Art (www.wga.hu) and Olga's Gallery (www.abcgallery.com), but many others can also be found by searching for virtual art galleries.

p. 19   viewing works of art "entails a contemplative waiting upon them": John Drury, *Painting the Word* (New Haven, Conn.: Yale University Press, 1999), pp. xiii, xiv.

Chapter 1: Awakening

p. 28   "We may ignore, but we can nowhere evade": C. S. Lewis, *Prayer: Letters to Malcolm* (Glasgow: Fontana Books, 1974), p. 77.

p. 33   "our eyes may perceive, yet they do not observe": Muriel Bar-
             bery, *The Elegance of the Hedgehog* (Paris: Editions Gallimard,
             2006), p. 304.

Chapter 2: Coming Aside
p. 37   a vacation with the Lord: Thomas H. Green, *A Vacation with
             the Lord* (Notre Dame, Ind.: Ave Maria Press, 1986).

Chapter 3: Gazing in Stillness
p. 46   "consent to the presence and action of God": Cynthia
             Bourgeault, *Centering Prayer and Inner Awakening* (Cambridge,
             Mass.: Cowley, 2004), pp. 24-25.

Chapter 4: Attuned to God's Presence
p. 57   "all your desire should be to praise God": Netta Peacock, *Millet*
             (New York: Dodge Publishing, 1905), p. 40.
p. 57   "paint for eternity": Ibid. p. 50.
p. 59   the man and the woman stand in bowed silence: Much has been
             written about the interpretation of this painting by Millet. The
             surrealist painter Salvador Dali suggested that the peasants
             were not praying the Angelus but were praying over their dead
             child, who was buried beneath their feet. An x-ray of the canvas
             later revealed what might be taken to be a coffin-like shape un-
             der the finished work, suggesting that the artist's original intent
             may have been different from his final version. However, the
             generally accepted view remains that the picture is a depiction
             of a couple praying the Angelus, and this academic dispute
             should not distract us from the spiritual reading of the painting
             which I offer.
p. 60   look into the face of God as I go through my day: See Thomas
             Green, *Opening to God: A Guide to Prayer* (Notre Dame, Ind.:
             Ave Maria Press, 1977), p. 31.
p. 61   "I feel simply carried along each hour": Frank Laubach, *Practic-
             ing His Presence* (Goleta, Calif.: Christian Books, 1976), p. 5.
p. 62   prayer is "an opening of the mind and heart to God": Green,
             Opening to God, p. 31.

Chapter 5: Called to See
p. 74   Christina Rossetti's "In the Bleak Midwinter": Christina Geor-
             gina Rossetti, Rebecca W. Crump and Betty S. Flowers, *Chris-*

tina Rosetti: The Complete Poems (London: Penguin Books, 2001), p. 210

p. 75   "To live within the near past-all-graspness of God": Karl Rhaner, *Prayers for a Lifetime* (New York: Crossroad Classics, 1995), p. 12.

Chapter 7: Seeing and Believing

p. 97   The poem "Wounded": John Shaw, "Wounded," in *A Widening Light: Poems of the Incarnation* (Wheaton, Ill.: Harold Shaw, 1984), p. 123.

Chapter 9: The Way of the Cross

p. 112   "we should push on into His presence": A. W. Tozer, *The Pursuit of God* (Camp Hill, Penn.: Christian Publications, 1993), p. 34.

p. 112   "May I know Thee more clearly": Richard of Chichester, quoted in Deborah Smith Douglas, *The Praying Life: Seeking God in All Things* (Harrisburg, Penn.: Morehouse Publishing, 2003), p. 34.

p. 120   "at the end there is always ultimate meaning": M. Basil Pennington, *Long on the Journey: The Reflections of a Pilgrim* (Huntington, Ind.: Our Sunday Visitor, 1989), p. 100.

Chapter 10: Called to Follow

p. 128   "Love given free of charge": Kathy Hughes, "Love with No Edges," *Facing the Shadow* (Christchurch, New Zealand: n.p., 2007), p. 21. Used with permission.

Chapter 13: Seeing and Serving

p. 160   "quivering of the heart in response to another's suffering": Mary Jo Meadows, *Gentling the Heart* (New York: Crossroad, 1994), p. 83.

p. 162   "Christ has no body now but yours": Teresa of Ávila, quoted in Michael E. Moynahan, *Once upon a Mystery: What Happens Next?* (New Jersey: Paulist Press, 2002), p. 43.

IMAGE CREDITS

Introduction
The Parable of the Blind, 1568 (tempera on canvas) by Bruegel, Pieter the Elder (c.1525-69). Museo e Gallerie Nazionali di Capodimonte, Naples, Italy/ Giraudon/The Bridgeman Art Library

Chapter 1
Census at Bethlehem, c.1566 (oil on panel) by Bruegel, Pieter the Elder (c.1525-69). Private Collection/The Bridgeman Art Library

Chapter 2
Christ in the Wilderness (oil on canvas) by Moretto da Brescia (1498-1554). The Metropolitan Museum of Art, New York, NY, USA. ©The Metropolitan Museum of Art/Art Resource, NY

Chapter 3 *(spot used on the front cover; full image used on the back cover)*
Christ in the House of Martha and Mary, c.1654-56 (oil on canvas), Vermeer, Jan (1632-75)/©National Gallery of Scotland, Edinburgh, Scotland/The Bridgeman Art Library

Chapter 4
The Angelus, 1857-59 (oil on canvas) by Millet, Jean-Francois (1814-75). Musee d'Orsay, Paris, France/Giraudon/The Bridgeman Art Library

Chapter 5
The Adoration of the Shepherds, c.1633-34 (oil on canvas) by Nicolas Poussin (1594-1665). National Gallery, London, Great Britain. Bought with a special grant and contribution from The Art Fund, 1957. © National Gallery, London/Art Resource, NY

Chapter 6
The Storm on the Sea of Galilee, 1633 (oil on canvas) by Rembrandt Harmensz. van Rijn (1606-69). © Isabella Stewart Gardner Museum, Boston, MA, USA/The Bridgeman Art Library

Chapter 7
Incredulity of St. Thomas, 1602-03 (oil on canvas) by Caravaggio, Michelangelo Merisi da (1571-1610). Schloss Sanssouci, Potsdam, Brandenburg, Germany/Alinari/The Bridgeman Art Library

Chapter 8
The Supper at Emmaus, 1601 (oil and tempera on canvas) by Caravaggio, Michelangelo Merisi da (1571-1610). National Gallery, London, UK/The Bridgeman Art Library

Chapter 9
The Procession to Calvary, c.1505 (oil on canvas transferred from wood) by Ghirlandaio, Ridolfo (Bigordi), Il (1483-1561). National Gallery, London, UK/The Bridgeman Art Library

Chapter 10
The Calling of St. Matthew, c.1598-1601 (oil on panel) by Caravaggio, Michelangelo Merisi da (1571-1610). Contarelli Chapel, S. Luigi dei Francesi, Rome, Italy/The Bridgeman Art Library

Chapter 11
The Visitation by He Qi <www.heqigallery.com>

Chapter 12
The Descent from the Cross, central panel of the triptych, 1611-14 (oil on panel) by Rubens, Peter Paul (1577-1640). Onze Lieve Vrouwkerk, Antwerp Cathedral, Belgium/The Bridgeman Art Library

Chapter 13
The Good Samaritan (oil on canvas) by Giordano, Luca (1634-1705). Musee des Beaux-Arts, Rouen, France/Lauros/Giraudon/The Bridgeman Art Library

formatio
TRADITION. EXPERIENCE.
TRANSFORMATION.

Formatio books from InterVarsity Press follow the rich tradition of the church in the journey of spiritual formation. These books are not merely about being informed, but about being transformed by Christ and conformed to his image. Formatio stands in InterVarsity Press's evangelical publishing tradition by integrating God's Word with spiritual practice and by prompting readers to move from inward change to outward witness. InterVarsity Press uses the chambered nautilus for Formatio, a symbol of spiritual formation because of its continual spiral journey outward as it moves from its center. We believe that each of us is made with a deep desire to be in God's presence. Formatio books help us to fulfill our deepest desires and to become our true selves in light of God's grace.

CONVER*sations*

A FORUM FOR *Authentic* TRANSFORMATION

Conversations is a semi-annual spiritual formation journal published by Richmont Graduate University. Each issue is devoted to a theme of Christian spiritual formation.

Our Purpose

The purpose of *Conversations* is to provide spiritual accompaniment and honest dialogue for those who long for radical transformation in Christ. It stimulates hunger and illuminates the path by drawing on classical wisdom and practice, exploring the vital role of community, and illustrating the journey with realism and hope.

Our Target Audience

The target audience for Conversations is purposefully broad—all thoughtful, seeking followers of Christ who long for a complete transformation of soul and full restoration of his image within. It is the intent of the editors to produce words that will inspire both those who seek help themselves and those who are helping others. The audience is also envisioned as being international, ecumenical and interdenominational.

Our Writers

Past conversations have included Dallas Willard, John Ortberg, Richard Foster, Emilie Griffin, David G. Benner, Mindy Caliguire, Gary W. Moon, Larry Crabb, Jan Johnson, Tara M. Owens, Keith Myers, Ruth Haley Barton and many others.

How to Join the *Conversation*

You're invited to join the conversation! To subscribe please visit our website conversationsjournal.com or call 800-607-4410. Get your "daily dose" of spiritual formation—discussion of issue themes, current events and honest accounts of others on this journey with you—at our blog, "The Daily Conversation."